The
Oxford
English
Programme

Use of
Language

2

John
O'Connor

Oxford University Press

Contents

INTRODUCTION

Books 1, 2 and 3 of *Use of Language* are designed for use in Years 7, 8, and 9 at Key Stage 3 or S1 and S2 in Scotland. Although the books concentrate especially upon Language in all its different forms, they actually cover much more. Every unit, for example, contains a 'feature text' most of which come from the world of literature.

People learn about language most easily and enjoyably when they can relate things to their own speech or writing or reading. That is why the activities ask you to use your own experience of language as the starting point.

The Contents Grid on pages 4-5 shows you how the book is made up. There are seven units and a Reference Section, which is followed by a Glossary.
● Each unit focuses upon a particular area of language. Unit 1, for example, is to do with where English words come from; Unit 7 looks at the differences between speaking and writing. Every unit ends with a special Language in Use activity which gives you the opportunity to put into practice what you have learned.
● Throughout the units there are sections on the different things that we can learn about language. These are to do with the important technical features of writing, such as punctuation, spelling, grammatical terms which help us to talk about language, reference skills, and the 'special effects' of language.
● The arrows on the Contents Grid show how these language features are linked to one another. Most of these features are returned to in The Reference Section

Each book is supported by a cassette of spoken material to be used alongside the activities in each unit. This includes not only readings of the feature texts and examples of accent and dialect, but also – in the belief that learning about language is as entertaining as it is useful – contributions from performers such as Victoria Wood.

John O'Connor

Contents Grid

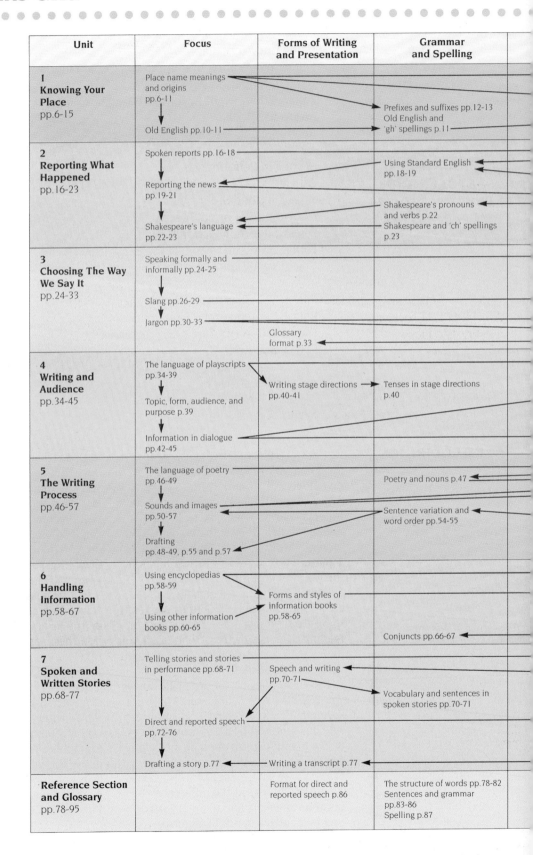

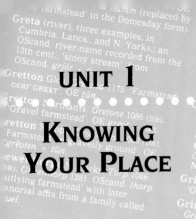

Greta (river), three examples, in Cumbria, Lancs, and N. Yorks.: an OScand. river-name recorded from the 13th cent. 'stony stream' from OScand. *griot*...

Gretton Gl... 1175. Farmstead near GREET. OE *tūn*...

Gretton Northants. *Gretone* 1086 (DB). 'Gravel farmstead.' OE *gréot*...

gretton Farmstead... 'gravelly ground.' OE ... *tūn*...

...thorp 1281. OScand. *thorp* 'outlying farmstead' with later manorial affix from a family called ...uel.

...rives an old bange...

, lytel spere, gif hit herinn...
Gif ðu wære on fell scote...
ðe wære on flæsc scote...
ðe wære on blod scoten,...
f hit wære ylfa gescot,...
ic wille þin helpan.

natural unnatura...

He said to me,
'Your tyres are getting a bit bald.'

me, 'where do you thi...
ng?' So I said, 'Nowh...

Nevertheless

And like

I   (On the moor)

(Thunder and lightning. Enter...

...rst Witch:
...hall we three meet again
...nder, lightning, or in rain?

...lly
the
...y!

This drink's warm... Put some Vincent... in, will you?

bolt

three-u...

...itement

Taste
The dry, musty le...
Which tamper w...
Lingering smok...

Where Do Place-names Come From?

What a place-name describes

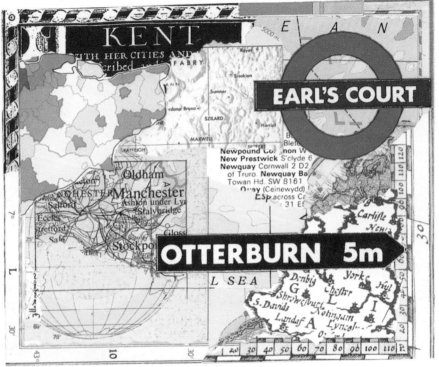

Does your town or village have an interesting name?
Have you ever wondered why it has that name? Or what it means?
Most counties, cities, towns and villages are named after:

- the *people* who once settled there – for example, *Suffolk* (the South folk)
- the kind of *settlement* they built – for example, *Upham* (the upper 'ham' or homestead)
- some interesting feature of the *landscape*

This might be a natural feature – for example, *Blackpool* or something that had been built – for example, *Newcastle*.

What do they mean?

How do you think the following places might have got their names? (You might need to use a dictionary to help with the meanings of 'burn' and 'scar'.)

- Castleton
- Kingsbridge
- Otterburn
- Southchurch
- Draperstown
- Ravenscar
- Newquay
- Greenford
- Wallsend (which wall?)

You can find the meanings of these place-names on page 88.

The people who invented the names

Most English place-names are over a thousand years old and were invented by three main groups of people.

The first group was the **Celts** (also known as Britons). They lived in the British Isles before the arrival of the Romans and gave us Celtic words such as:

Devon and *Leeds* – named after the Celtic tribes that lived there

Kent 'the area by the coast'   *York* 'yew-tree estate'

Avon   'river'   *Exe* 'the water'

Thames – which probably means 'dark'

Many Scottish, Welsh, and Irish place-names come from the Celtic languages of the original inhabitants.

For more about these place-names see The Reference Section page 80.

It was the **Anglo-Saxons** (who came from northern Europe in the Fifth century) who invented most of the place-names that we use today. We call their language Old English. Some of their words are found at the ends of many of our place-names. For example:

-stow   a 'holy place' or 'meeting place'   *-wick* or *-wich*   'farm'

-bury, *-burgh*, *-borough* and *-brough*   a 'stronghold' or 'fortified place'

Old English words usually found at the beginnings of place-names include:

Swin- 'swine' or 'pigs'   *Ship-* 'sheep'   *Lang-* 'long'

Whit- 'white'   *Prest-* 'priest'

The third group of settlers to invent new place-names were the **Vikings** from Norway and Denmark. Their language was Old Scandinavian and it gives us parts of place-names such as:

-thwaite –'clearing' or 'meadow'   *-toft* – 'homestead'

-kirk – 'church'

And what about the Romans? You can find out about Roman place-names on page 78 of The Reference Section.

CREATING PLACE-NAMES

In pairs, try putting some of these parts of place-names together and see whether you end up with real place-names. For example, do Shipton ('sheep settlement') and Langthwaite ('long clearing') really exist?

You can check by looking in the Gazeteer (index) of an atlas.

Discovering Meanings

. . . .

WORKING OUT THE MEANINGS

1 Use the information in and around this dictionary extract from *A Dictionary of English Place-Names* and the panel of information on page 9 to complete the chart on the opposite page.

Gressingham

(DB). 'Grassy or gravelly nook of land'. OE *gærsen or grēosn + halh.

Gressingham Lancs. *Ghersinctune* 1086 (DB), *Gersingeham* 1183. 'Homestead or enclosure with grazing or pasture'. OE *gærsing + hām or hamm (replaced by tūn 'farmstead' in the Domesday form).

Greta (river), three examples, in Cumbria, Lancs., and N. Yorks.; an OScand. river-name recorded from the 13th cent., 'stony stream', from OScand. grjót + á.

Gretton Glos. *Gretona* 1175. 'Farmstead near GREET'. OE tūn.

Gretton Northants. *Gretone* 1086 (DB). 'Gravel farmstead'. OE grēot + tūn.

Gretton Shrops. *Grotintune* 1086 (DB). 'Farmstead on gravelly ground'. OE *grēoten + tūn.

Grewelthorpe N. Yorks. *Torp* 1086 (DB), *Gruelthorp* 1281. OScand. thorp 'outlying farmstead' with later manorial affix from a family called *Gruel*.

Greysouthen Cumbria. *Craykesuthen* c.1187. 'Rock or cliff of a man called Suthán'. Celtic *creig + OIrish pers. name.

Greystoke Cumbria. *Creistoc* 1167. Probably 'secondary settlement by a river once called *Cray*'. Lost Celtic river-name (meaning 'fresh, clean') + OE stoc.

Greywell Hants. *Graiwella* 1167. Probably 'spring or stream frequented by badgers'. OE *græg + wella.

Griff Warwicks. *Griva* 12th cent. '(Place at) the deep valley or hollow'. OScand. gryfja.

Grimley Heref. & Worcs. *Grimanleage* 9th cent., *Grimanleh* 1086 (DB). 'Wood or glade haunted by a spectre or goblin'. OE grīma + lēah.

Grimoldby Lincs. *Grimoldbi* 1086 (DB). 'Farmstead or village of a man called Grimald'. OGerman pers. name + OScand. bý.

Grimsargh Lancs. *Grimesarge* 1086 (DB). 'Hill-pasture of a man called Grímr'. OScand. pers. name + erg.

Grimsby, 'farmstead or village of a man called Grímr', OScand. pers. name + bý: **Grimsby** Humber. *Grimesbi* 1086

Grinton

(DB). **Grimsby, Little** Lincs. *Grimesbi* 1086 (DB).

Grimscote Northants. *Grimescote* 12th cent. 'Cottage(s) of a man called Grímr'. OScand. pers. name + OE cot.

Grimstead, East & West Wilts. *Gremestede* 1086 (DB). Probably 'green homestead'. OE grēne + hām-stede.

Grimsthorpe Lincs. *Grimestorp* 1212. 'Outlying farmstead or hamlet of a man called Grímr' OScand. pers. name + thorp.

Grimston, 'farmstead or estate of a man called Grímr', OScand. pers. name + OE tūn; examples include: **Grimston** Leics. *Grimestone* 1086 (DB). **Grimston** Norfolk. *Grimastun* c.1035, *Grimestuna* 1086 (DB). **Grimston, North** N. Yorks. *Grimeston* 1086 (DB).

Grindale Humber. *Grendele* 1086 (DB). 'Green valley'. OE grēne + dæl.

Grindleton Lancs. *Gretlintone* 1086 (DB) *Grenlington* 1251. Probably 'farmstead near the gravelly stream'. OE *grendel + -ing + tūn.

Grindley Staffs. *Grenleg* 1251. 'Green woodland clearing'. OE grēne + lēah.

Grindlow Derbys. *Grenlawe* 1199. 'Green hill or mound'. OE grēne + hlāw.

Grindon, 'green hill', OE grēne + dūn: **Grindon** Northum. *Grandon* 1210. **Grindon** Staffs. *Grendone* 1086 (DB).

Gringley on the Hill Notts. *Gringeleia* 1086 (DB). Possibly 'woodland clearing of the people living at the green place'. OE grēne + -inga- + lēah.

Grinsdale Cumbria. *Grennesdale* c.1180. Probably 'valley by the green promontory'. OE grēne + næss + OScand. dalr.

Grinshill Shrops. *Grivelesul (sic)* 1086 (DB), *Grineleshul* 1242. OE hyll 'hill' with an uncertain first element.

Grinstead, 'green place' i.e. 'pasture used for grazing', OE grēne + stede: **Grinstead, East** W. Sussex. *Grenesteda* 1121, *Estgrenested* 1271. **Grinstead, West** W. Sussex. *Grenestede* 1086 (DB), *Westgrenested* 1280.

Grinton N. Yorks. *Grinton* 1086 (DB). 'Green farmstead'. OE grēne + tūn.

Annotations (handwritten):

The meaning of the name.

The earliest recorded spelling.

The date when the name was first recorded. (DB) means that the name is in the Domesday Book.

The language or languages which the name came from. This one is from Old English.

The first and second parts of this name are from Old English; the third from Old Scandinavian.

Both parts of this name are from Old Scandinavian.

A. D. Mills

Names in two parts

As you have seen, many English place-names were made up by putting two words together. A place where there was a ford where oxen crossed might be called *Ox-ford*. Other examples are *South-gate* and *Whit-church*.

Names with people in them

Sometimes the first part of the place-name is the name of the Viking or Anglo-Saxon man or woman who was the first to settle there. *Kenilworth* is 'the enclosure (*worth*) of a woman called Cynehild'.

Names in three parts

A place-name such as *Framlingham* is actually made up of three words. The middle part, *-ing* often means 'the followers of', so Framl*ing*ham becomes 'the homestead of the followers of a man called Framela'.

Make your own copy of this chart. Filling it in will help you to build up a good understanding of how English place-names have been formed and then to work out others on your own.

Old word found in place-names	Its meaning	The language it came from	Example
ham	homestead	....	Gressingham
ton	....	Old English	....
....	outlying farmstead	Old Scandinavian	....
hill	....		
stead	....	....	Grinstead
....	cottage	....	....
by	....	....	Grimsby
well	....	....	
don	....		Grindon
ley	wood or glade	....	....
....	secondary settlement	....	....
dale	....	Old English	....
....	hill or mound	....	Grindlow

2 Look back over this unit to find out how the places below got their names. Write explanations similar to those in A *Dictionary of English Place-names*, but leave out dates and other details that you could not be expected to know. Check your ideas with the origins on page 88.
- Prestwich
- Whitby
- Shipley
- Langdon
- Norfolk
- Boroughbridge
- Swinstead
- Birmingham (Birm- from an Anglo-Saxon man called 'Beorma')

3 Write a short story describing how a place got its name. You could invent your own place-name or use one of these. (The actual meanings are on page 88. But write your own story before looking them up.)
- Ottery Saint Mary
- Toller Porcorum
- Eye

Your story might be about the person who gave his or her name to the place. For example, *Greysouthen* means 'the rock or cliff of a man called Suthan'.

What kind of person was he? Why should they name a cliff after him? What happened at *Grimley* (which means 'wood or glade haunted by a spectre or goblin')?

Old English

Old English, as you have learned, is the name we give to the language spoken by the Anglo-Saxons. You have already met some Old English words.

Use the extract from the place-names dictionary on page 8 to find out the meanings of Old English:

tun   wella   leah   dun   grene

What were the Old English words for:

a homestead   a secondary settlement   a cottage
a goblin   gravel   a valley   a promontary?

A magic charm

Do you carry anything around with you for luck? Or have you got a special remedy for hiccups or nettle stings?
The Anglo-Saxons had charms and remedies for all sorts of things.

At some time or other you must have had a sharp pain in your side when you were running. We call it a 'stitch', which comes from the Old English word *stice* (pronounced 'stitcher'). The Anglo-Saxons described stitch as a 'little spear' and had a special charm to cure it. This charm involves collecting some common plants which include *reade netele* (red nettle), which is said to grow *þurh* (through) the house. They are then boiled up in some *buteran* (butter).
Meanwhile you say these words.

Letters
ð and þ =th
(ðu = 'thou' or 'you'
and þin ='thine' or 'you')
æ = e
sc = sh
u = ou (or: ow)
ignore g and ge at the beginning of words

Words
hit = 'it'
herinne = 'herein' (or: 'in here')
sie = 'is'
fell = 'skin'
oððe = 'or'
ylfa = 'of elves'

Phrases
on fell scoten = 'shot in the skin' (literally 'on skin shot'

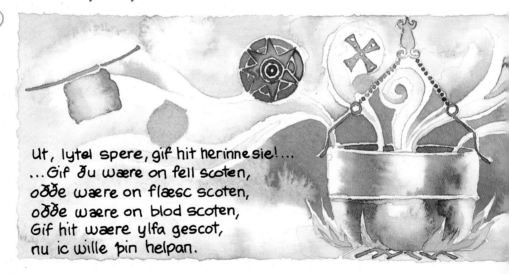

Ut, lytel spere, gif hit herinne sie!...
...Gif ðu wære on fell scoten,
oððe wære on flæsc scoten,
oððe wære on blod scoten,
Gif hit wære ylfa gescot,
nu ic wille þin helpan.

The final part of the charm involves plunging your knife into the boiled up plant-and-butter mixture!

WORDS FROM OLD ENGLISH

1   See how much of the charm you can translate, using the notes given around the charm.

2   How difficult did you find the charm to understand? Make a list of:
   ● the words which look different to modern English, but can still be worked out
   ● the words which are not recognizable at all
   There are 21 different words in the passage. Although the spellings and the sounds of the words have changed, they are nearly all to be found in our modern English. A translation of the charm is given on page 88.

READING OLD ENGLISH

1   Listen to the reading of the whole charm on the cassette.
   It is difficult to describe Old English sounds in modern English spelling, but the beginning of the charm might be represented something like this:
   Oot, lutel spaier, yif hit hairinner zee!
   Yif thoo warrer on fell shotten other warrer on flash…

2   In pairs, try reading the charm out loud. Each take one line in turn. Then compare your reading with the one on the cassette.

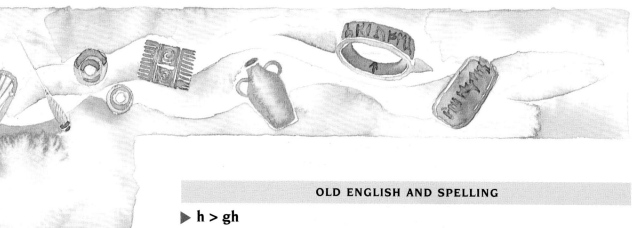

OLD ENGLISH AND SPELLING

▶ **h > gh**
One of the plants required for the charm was red nettle, which grows *þurh* (through) the house. Over the centuries the final **-h** has become **-gh.** For more examples, see page 87 of The Reference Section.
How do we now spell the following Old English words?
niht dohtor broht noht hihte

Building Words

Most English place-names, as you have seen, are formed by adding two words or word-parts together. *New* and *quay* are joined together to make the name *Newquay*, for example.

In English we often do something like this with other kinds of words and word-parts too.

Prefixes

In Book 1, Unit 1 you learned about *negative prefixes*: groups of letters added to the beginnings of words in order to give them an opposite meaning:

- natural - *un*natural
- legal - *il*legal

Prefix is from Latin and means 'something fixed in front'.

Prefixes occur in words all the time. Many of them are from Latin or Ancient Greek words. *Aqua-* in *Aquarium*, for example, comes from a Latin word meaning 'water'; *cent-* in *cent*ipede means 'a hundred'.

SPOT THE PREFIX

The signs in this air terminal include more than 20 prefixes. Make a list of these, saying what each one means and providing at least one further example of each. Compare your list with the one on pages 81-82 of The Reference Section.

Suffixes

Suffixes are single letters or groups of letters joined to the ends of words or word-parts. Prefixes and suffixes are known as **affixes**.

SUFFIX-PHOBIA

1 The printer attached to this word-processor has developed a strange fault known as 'suffix-phobia', which prevents it from printing certain suffixes. Decide which ones could be added so the memo makes sense.

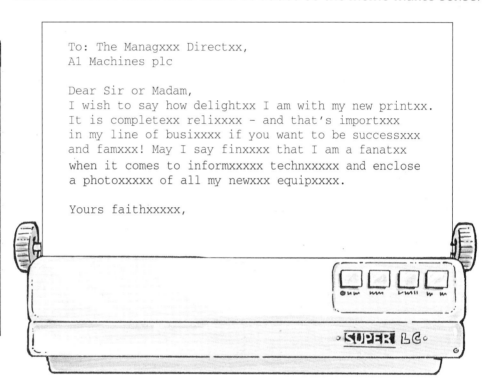

```
To: The Managxxx Directxx,
A1 Machines plc

Dear Sir or Madam,
I wish to say how delightxx I am with my new printxx.
It is completexx relixxxx - and that's importxxx
in my line of busixxxx if you want to be successxxx
and famxxx! May I say finxxxx that I am a fanatxx
when it comes to informxxxxx technxxxxx and enclose
a photoxxxxx of all my newxxx equipxxxx.

Yours faithxxxxx,
```

LANGUAGE DATABASE

▶ **Suffixes**

A letter or group of letters joined to the end of a word in order to make it into a different word class:
e.g. quick quick*ly*
excite excite*ment*
sand sand*y*
or to create a new word by joining with a prefix
e.g. tele-phone
bi-ology centi-metre

2 Use a word-processor to input your own piece of writing with suffix-phobia. Then ask a partner to cure it by adding appropriate suffixes.

'HE'S GOT AN -OLOGY!'

What does the suffix *-ology* (or *-logy*) mean? At the moment you are thinking about **etymology**. This is *the study of* where words come from and how they are made up. The word itself comes from the Greek *etymon* meaning 'original word' and *logia* meaning 'study'.

1 How many *-logys* can you think of?
2 Which *-logys* mean the study of:
   ● the mind   ● human beings   ● the Earth   ● animals?

Place-names in Poetry

 Here are two very different ways in which people have chosen to write about place-names. The first is a poem, the second the lyrics of a well-known pop song. You will find them both on the cassette.

Adlestrop

Yes. I remember Adlestrop –
The name, because one afternoon
Of heat the express-train drew up there
Unwontedly. It was late June.

The steam hissed. Someone cleared his throat.
No one left and no one came
On that bare platform. What I saw
Was Adlestrop – only the name

And willows, willow-herb, and grass,
And meadowsweet, and haycocks dry,
No whit less still and lonely fair
Than the high cloudlets in the sky.

And for that minute a blackbird sang
Close by, and round him, mistier,
Farther and farther, all the birds
Of Oxfordshire and Gloucestershire.

Edward Thomas

Route 66

…It winds from Chicago to LA,
More than two thousand miles all the way.
Get your kicks on Route 66!

Now you go through Saint Looey and Joplin, Missouri
And Oklahoma City is mighty pretty
You'll see Amarillo; Gallup, New Mexico;
Flagstaff, Arizona;
Don't forget Winona,
Kingman, Barstow, San Bernadino…

Bobby Troup

CELEBRATING PLACE-NAMES

1   Write a poem which 'celebrates' the place-names of your own region. It might be something thought-provoking like *Adlestrop* or simply a poem that brings together the wonderful sounds of different names, as *Route 66* does.

2   Try to find other poems or song lyrics which seem to be about places and their names. Your library will probably have anthologies which contain John Betjeman's *Essex*, A.E. Housman's *Wenlock Edge*, or Stevie Smith's *Harold's Leap*. There are hundreds of songs too, including *Penny Lane* and *Strawberry Fields* by Lennon and McCartney.

3   Because place-names have meanings, it is easy to form pictures of them in our minds. For example, there is a place in Somerset called Queen Camel!
Try drawing your own illustrations of interesting place-names and build up an amusing wall display. (Do you live near Greenhead, for example? Or Hatfield, Snailwell or Sheepwash?)

LANGUAGE IN USE

Make up a simplified Dictionary of Local Place-names for use in one of your nearby primary schools. Remember to use language which is appropriate to your audience (see Book 1, Unit 4). You might like to word-process your work and make it into a booklet. Witty illustrations would also add to the appeal for younger children.

It Happened at School…

In this unit we will look at some of the ways in which different people give spoken accounts of things that have happened.

Your account

Working in pairs, tell each other a true story about an incident at school. This account is not for a public audience – only for your partner. It might be about something that happened:

- in class
- on the games field
- or in the playground

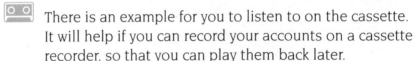 There is an example for you to listen to on the cassette. It will help if you can record your accounts on a cassette recorder, so that you can play them back later.

Someone else's account

In this extract from *My Mate Shofiq*, the narrator is telling us about the time when Bernard Kershaw found himself waiting outside the Head's office with another boy from his class, Shofiq Rahman.

 My Mate Shofiq

On his way to school that morning, Bernard had witnessed the normally quiet Shofiq go into a blind fury. He was defending his little sisters from a gang of bullies led by a boy called Bobby Whitehead. Bernard had told his class teacher but is less keen to talk to the Head, Mr Ellis, and begins to make excuses to get back to his class…

'I never seen nothing really,' he said once, hopefully, to the boy. 'I were miles away. Right over the croft.'

…The Pakistani lad lifted up his fist and banged on the door as bold as brass. In the interval before the Headmaster replied he smiled again.

'You'll be champion,' he said. 'Give over worrying.'

The first thing that Bernard saw, when the order came and this Shofiq pushed the door open, was bad enough. Mr Ellis was standing behind his desk, not sitting, and he looked like a dirty great thundercloud.

…The Pakistani lad's voice, when it came, shocked him. It was quiet, and polite, and firm. He didn't sound scared, he didn't sound worried, he didn't sound anything.

I don't know what he's told you already, sir,' he said, nodding towards Whitehead, 'but this is what happened. My two little sisters, sir, that are in the infants, have been getting a bit of stick, sir. On their way to school, like. Two or three times last week, once the week before, lots of times before that, on and off.'

'Stick?' said Mr Ellis nastily. 'You mean the cane has been applied in the infants' school? That is a most unlikely allegation.'

There was a fairly long pause. The Pakistani lad didn't move. Out of the corner of his eye Bernard could see him looking at the Headmaster. It was just typical of Ellis to take it wrong. He was a stickler for proper English…

…The Pakistani lad went on, as calm as ever.

'Sorry, sir. I mean, that on their way to school they've had a bit of trouble, sir. With some lads. With that lad Whitehead there. And his gang.

…My sister, the youngest one, sir, has got a cut face from last week. It upsets my mother, sir. She doesn't understand. Little friends too, sir. They usually come to school in a bunch, about half a dozen, sir. Today, I followed them.'

Bernard stole a glance at Bobby Whitehead. He looked proper ill.

'So when you attacked Robert Whitehead, you did it to prevent an attack upon your sister?'

'After, sir. After an attack on my sisters. Two of them, sir.'

'Ah,' said Mr Ellis. 'So you do admit that you attacked this boy?'

'Oh yes, sir. I found a piece of rubber hose and I hit him with it. I was a bit feared at first, in case I'd killed him, sir, but he seemed all right, lying in the puddle. Dead people don't bleed you know, sir. And he were bleeding right fast.'

Jan Needle

TALKING ABOUT THE ISSUES

My Mate Shofiq deals with the issue of racism. In a group, discuss whether, in your opinion, the narrator seems to be racist. Look at the ways in which he refers to Shofiq, for example, but also the ways in which he describes Shofiq's behaviour in the presence of Mr Ellis.

LOOKING AT THE LANGUAGE

1   Sometimes people in authority use language to make others feel inferior or to make themselves feel important. In pairs, find some examples which show Mr Ellis using language in this way.
    Where, for example, does he use 'formal' vocabulary, when more everyday words would do?

    Where in the extract would you say Mr Ellis stops using language like this and actually begins to communicate properly with the boys?

2   The narrator says that Mr Ellis is 'a stickler for proper English'. Whenever Bernard and Shofiq speak, they use words and phrases from their own dialect. For example Bernard says, 'I never seen nothing' and 'I were miles away.'
    List three or four other examples of Bernard's and Shofiq's language which are not *Standard English dialect*. (To remind yourself about Standard English, you may find it useful to look it up on page 94.)
    Are these expressions that you would use?

3   What do you think of Shofiq's use of non-standard dialect?
    Discuss it with your partner:
    Is his account more interesting and varied because of it, or less so?
    Is it harder to understand or easier?
    Does it make no difference at all?

TALKING ABOUT YOUR OWN LANGUAGE

Now go back to your own accounts from page 16 and talk about the kind of language that you used. It will help to listen to your tape recordings again first.

1   Did you tell your story completely in Standard English dialect or did you use some words and phrases from a local dialect?

2   Most importantly, was the language you used varied and original? Did it make your story interesting to listen to?

Reporting the News

One group of people who nearly always use Standard English in their reporting are radio and television news-readers.

This is because Standard English is thought to be a 'neutral' dialect. In other words, it does not 'belong' to:
- any particular part of the country or
- any one of the English-speaking countries around the world.

(It is important to remember, though, that different countries, like the United States, have their own standard forms of the language, which are different from British Standard English.)

Reading the report

Read and listen to the following radio news item about the Oscar Awards Ceremony in Hollywood:

It was celebration time for the home film industry in Hollywood last night as Britain scooped no fewer than five Oscars at the prestigious annual awards ceremony. Emma Thompson collected the best actress award for her part in *Howards End*, the British film which also won honours for Best Art Direction and Best Adapted Screenplay. Although hot favourite for the award, Miss Thompson told the star-studded audience, 'It just takes my breath away.' Further successes for Britain came in the shape of the Best Original Screenplay award for director Neil Jordan's *The Crying Game*, a controversial film about the IRA, and for lyricist Tim Rice who shared the award for Best Original Song. The night was also a special one for veteran actor and director Clint Eastwood, named Best Director for his hard-hitting western, *Unforgiven*. This was Eastwood's first Oscar in 39 years of film-making.

LOOKING AT THE STRUCTURE

Many radio and television news items are put together like the one above. Although they might read like natural speech, they are carefully planned out. Look carefully at the Oscars news item to see how it has been constructed.

If we were turning this into a written piece, how many paragraphs would there be?

Draw up a plan, giving each paragraph a heading and adding a brief phrase or two to describe what each paragraph is saying.

When you have completed it, compare your plan with a partner's.

Then compare both with the suggested plan on pages 88-89.

And earlier today on the battlements of Elsinore Castle.....

1   In groups of four, read and then act out the following cartoon strip, which tells of a mysterious and frightening moment in which a ghost appears to three young men. The incident is from the opening of Shakespeare's play, *Hamlet*. You can hear a reading of this extract on the cassette.

The scene takes place on the battlements of Elsinore Castle, Denmark. It is the middle of a freezing night, two months after the sudden death of the King. As the guardsman Barnardo begins to tell his friend Horatio about the ghost which appeared on the castle battlements the night before, he is interrupted by Marcellus, who has caught sight of the spectre once again…

1. Peace, break thee off. Look where it comes again.

In the same figure like the king that's dead.

2. Thou art a scholar, speak to it, Horatio.

Looks it not like the king? Mark it, Horatio.

Most like. It harrows me with fear and wonder.

3. It would be spoke to.

Question it, Horatio.

4. What art thou that usurp'st this time of night Together with that fair and warlike form In which the majesty of buried Denmark Did sometimes march?

2 Imagine that Horatio has taken his story to Radio Elsinore FM.
   In your groups, prepare a radio news report of this incident.
   Think about the language of the Oscars report and the way in which
   the item was planned.
   You might include:
   - an account of what seems to have happened (setting the scene
     giving a sense of the atmosphere)
   - some background information (e.g. about the recent sudden death
     of the King)
   - statements from Barnardo, Marcellus, and Horatio
   - predictions about what this vision of the ghost means
     (including the opinion of an 'expert' in the supernatural)

3 When you have prepared and rehearsed your script, record it, sharing
   out the parts of the news-reader and the other voices.

WHAT HAPPENS NEXT?

In the same groups, discuss what you think might happen after this
incident, which is the very first thing the audience sees in the play.
Do you know what happens in the rest of *Hamlet* already? If you are
interested you could act out more of the play in groups or watch one
of the film versions, such as the production starring Mel Gibson.

Shakespeare's Language

Shakespeare wrote *Hamlet* almost four centuries ago and, not surprisingly, the English language has changed in that time. But has it changed that much? The main differences are probably to do with vocabulary, pronouns, and the endings of verbs.

TAKING A CLOSER LOOK

Discuss the following areas of Shakespeare's language, with a partner.

Unfamiliar vocabulary

Use a dictionary to look up any words in the cartoon strip on pages 20-21 which are unfamiliar to you. You will find that words, such as *usurp* and *harrow*, are still in use today, though they are not met very often.

Familiar words used in less familiar ways

Mark, *fair*, and *charge* are all common words in modern English and they can all be used with the same meanings as they had in Shakespeare's time. Today, though, they usually have slightly different meanings. Write down:
- their meanings in this extract
- their more usual modern meanings

Shakespeare's pronouns

Which two pronouns did people use in Shakespeare's time where we might use *you* (when speaking to one person)? In fact, these words came from the Old English þu or ðu, which you will remember from the charm for 'stitch' on page 10.

Shakespeare's verbs

Look at these phrases which contain verbs.
break thee off
Thou art a scholar
Looks it not like the king?
It would be spoke to.
What art thou...?
...that usurp'st...
Did sometimes march
I charge thee speak

Write each one out as it would appear in modern English and then explain exactly what the differences are. When you have finished, compare your versions with the ones on page 89.

▶ –ch pattern

The **–ch** combination of letters in T*hou art a s*ch*olar*... is quite common in English, but it is not usually pronounced with the 'hard' sound that we hear in 'scholar'.

Make three lists under these headings:

● words which begin with the 'soft' *ch* sound (as in *cheese*)
● words which end in *ch* or *tch* (as in *catch*)
● words in which *ch* has a 'hard' sound (as in *scholar*)

There are some examples of these on page 87 of The Reference Section.

LANGUAGE IN USE

In groups of four or five, prepare a complete ten-minute radio news programme.

You might base it upon

● School news: 'Holtley School is today reeling after the Head's shock decision... '
● News from your local community: 'It now looks certain that the Holtley Youth Club... '
● Incidents from a book that you are all reading in class: 'And the agricultural world tonight is still stunned by the daring and spectacular animal revolution at Manor Farm... '
● Events from a particular period in history: 'The newsdesk is just receiving reports of a fleet of Spanish ships...'

Remember that each news item has to be carefully planned. You may wish to work individually on the items or in pairs.

When it comes to the practising and recording, it will help if each member of the team has a particular role or roles. One or two people could be the main news-readers, for example, others the voices of the various people interviewed.

UNIT 3

CHOOSING THE WAY WE SAY IT

Speaking Formally and Informally

 There is something not quite right about this television news item. Read it through and then listen to it on the cassette.

> There was a terrific bust-up in the Commons today after the PM had got into a row over the Common Market. He got a bit peeved after the Leader of the Opposition had taken the mickey out of his policies for jobs, and then went more or less completely bananas when some character reckoned he was pretty clueless about inflation too. Anyway, the Speaker got stuck in and they patched it up before anybody drew blood, so all's well that ends well, I suppose.

FINDING THE INFORMAL

The language used here is informal and we normally expect formal spoken English from a news presenter, as was seen in Unit 2.

In pairs, pick out the phrases which seem to be particularly out of place. Then work out a more likely formal version of the same report – one that you could reasonably expect to hear on television – and record it.

Compare your recordings with those of other pairs and discuss the choices that you made concerning the language. Focus on the changes you made to:
- vocabulary
- phrases

USING FORMAL AND INFORMAL SPEECH

Still in pairs, list three situations in which you would normally use formal speech and three in which you would speak informally. (You may not always use formal speech in certain situations and always use informal speech in others. So add three other situations which you are really not certain about.) Share your ideas as a class and then look at the suggestions on page 89.

Knowing when to use informal language

In the extract from *My Mate Shofiq* in on pages 16-17, there is a moment when Shofiq tells the Headmaster, Mr Ellis, that his little sisters have been 'getting a bit of stick'. Mr Ellis pretends that he does not understand:

> 'Stick?' said Mr Ellis nastily. 'You mean the cane has been applied in the infants' school?'

With your partner, look back at the extract and discuss Mr Ellis' response. Why does he say that? What is the narrator's opinion of Mr Ellis' comment? What is your opinion?

In fact, Mr Ellis understands perfectly well what Shofiq means. But he wants to let him know that 'getting a bit of stick' is the kind of expression that young people should use only among themselves (if at all) and that Shofiq should have chosen a more formal expression when speaking to his Headmaster.

Slang

We call a phrase like 'getting a bit of stick' a **slang** expression.

Here are ten comments about slang. Give each one a mark out of five (5 = you strongly agree, 0 = you strongly disagree). Then compare your marks in groups of four and finally try to arrive at a definition of what slang is.

Slang is a lazy way of speaking.

You use slang to be fashionable.

People use slang to avoid speaking in a 'posh' way.

People use slang because they can't speak proper English.

Slang is used for fun.

Slang makes people take notice of what you are saying.

Slang makes the language more interesting.

You can picture things more easily when people describe them using slang.

Slang is useful when you don't want to be too serious.

I can get on with my friends better if I use slang.

LANGUAGE DATABASE

▶ **Slang**

A special form of language used in informal situations. Slang can be funny and striking and is sometimes used to show that we belong to a particular group:
e.g. taking a bit of stick
he drives an old banger
my plates are killing me

WHEN DO WE USE SLANG?

There is nothing 'lazy' or 'wrong' about using slang, but, as with all kinds of language, we do have to use it at the right moments. *Slang* is normally used in informal situations.

Choose any three of the informal situations from your list from page 25 and give examples of a slang expression that might arise in each one. For example:

Situation: You are with friends and spot a teacher coming.

Slang expression: 'Quick. Leg it!'

WHO USES IT?

Everybody uses slang at some time or another. But certain kinds of slang are usually used only among special groups. For example, young people in the 1950s described their music as 'cool' and the older generation as 'square'.

1   In pairs, make a list of some of the slang expressions which you and your friends use or which you have often heard. Then give the meaning of each one.
    To start you off, you might like to think about some examples of school slang.
    Important: Do not for the moment include any which might offend other people, such as swear words or racist expressions. (You should ask your teacher's advice about this.)

2   When you have completed your list, compare it with other pairs'.
    ● Are there certain expressions which some people feel are now out of date, but which other people still use?
    ● Do you have any on your list which the others have never heard of?

3   Finally, discuss in groups what main differences there are between *slang* expressions (such as 'a bit of stick') and *dialect* expressions (such as 'You'll be champion.')? Check your ideas with the ones on page 89.

WHY DO WE USE SLANG?

1   Choose five of your slang expressions and, for each one, decide whether any of the following statements is true:
    ● 'It is a more lively and interesting expression than the formal English version.'
    ● 'When I use it, it makes me feel part of a group.'
    ● 'This is a new, fashionable expression; using it is like wearing fashionable clothes.'
    ● 'It makes people laugh.'

2   What do your ideas about these statements tell you about the main reasons why you use slang?

Rhyming Slang

Rhyming slang was invented by Cockneys from London (possibly as a 'secret' language to mystify outsiders), but, with television programmes such as *Minder* and *EastEnders*, some expressions are now heard everywhere.

HOW DOES IT WORK?

Rhyming slang is something that has to be spoken and heard rather than written down. In rhyming slang, a phrase is invented which rhymes with the word that it stands for. For example:

- stairs are called *apples and pears*
- feet are *plates of meat*
- bed is *Uncle Ned*

1   Discuss in groups of three what you think the following rhyming slang expressions might mean:
- 'I've torn me round the houses.'
- 'Hello, my currant bun.'
- 'This is Julie, my skin and blister.'
- 'I'm feeling a bit Uncle Dick.'
- 'What a north and south!'

Just to make things more interesting (and harder for strangers to understand) the second part of the phrase is usually left out.
For example:
'My plates are killing me. It's running up and down those apples.'

 2   In pairs, listen to the conversation in rhyming slang, called 'Would You Adam and Eve It?', on the cassette. List the examples you hear and work out their meanings. You can check your answers on page 89.

NEW RHYMING SLANG

All of the expressions that you have met so far have been around for a long time.
But the exciting thing about rhyming slang is that new examples are being invented every day. Many of these are based upon the names of well-known people. What might a *Michael Caine* be?

1   See how many of the following you can work out.
    The answers are on page 89.

2   Make up your own new examples of rhyming slang, based upon well-known people. What, for example, might a *Kenneth Branagh* be? When you try out your new expressions, remember that you should only use the first half of the new phrase.

    There is no reason why rhyming slang has to belong to Londoners, as this example from Glasgow shows: *Winners and Loosers = troosers.*

Jargon

Jargon is the name we give to the special words used by particular groups of people who share the same job or interest.

WHAT'S YOUR HOBBY?

1 Think about any sport, pastime, or hobby that you enjoy and list five words or phrases which 'belong' to it. (For example, if you know something about tennis, you might list *deuce*, *love*, *let*, *service*, and *foot fault*.) Try to pick some of the more unusual expressions.

2 When you have completed your list, challenge a partner to explain some of your jargon.

The uses of jargon

There are two good reasons for using jargon. It can be a very helpful short cut and it can also help you to make explanations more precise.

JARGON AS A SHORT CUT

1 Take one of the jargon words or phrases that your partner found difficult and:
- use it in a short sentence
- write out a careful explanation of its meaning

For example, you might write:

> It was exciting when the players reached *deuce*.
> *Deuce*: The score in tennis when both players (or pairs) have 40 points and need to gain two successive points to win the game.

Now write the example sentence again but, instead of using jargon, include the explanation:

> It was exciting when they reached *the score where both players had 40 points and needed to gain two successive points to win the game.*

This should show how jargon can be useful as a handy short cut.

2 In pairs, think of situations where people forget the jargon and have to use the longer explanation instead. Draw some humorous cartoons like this to illustrate what happens.

LANGUAGE DATABASE

▶ **Jargon**

The technical or specialist terms used by a particular group, such as sportspeople, computer users or carpenters:
e.g. She managed a *birdie* on the fourth
I can't *access* the data
You need a *mortice and tenon* joint there.

And Davies is in one of those positions where he can't hit a colour he wants without hitting another colour accidentally first and giving four points away.

If you mean I'm 'snookered', say so!

JARGON TO BE PRECISE

In this situation, the correct use of jargon would not merely be a short cut: it would also tell the nurse exactly what was wanted at a critical moment.

How many other situations can you list in which using the correct piece of jargon is crucially important?

JARGON TO MYSTIFY PEOPLE

It is never a good idea to use jargon when you are talking to people who might not understand it. It simply confuses them and makes them feel left out.

Sometimes words used as jargon in a particular job or activity are borrowed from another language. Which activity are these words associated with? Do you know any of their meanings? You can check them in a dictionary.

● *sonata* ● *andante* ● *pianissimo* ● *crescendo* ● *da capo*

Birdies, Eagles, and Bogeys

These extracts from newspaper golf reports are full of the kind of jargon which can be quite mystifying if you do not happen to know much about the subject.

LOOKING AT THE JARGON

In pairs, make a list of all the words and phrases which you would class as jargon and then discuss their meanings. (Some of them have been highlighted in the first report.) Which terms do you happen to know already? Which ones can you work out from the context?

Alfredsson gets clear in the Open

Helen Alfredsson took a two-stroke lead into the last round of the US Women's Open when she fired a **three-under-par** 69 to give her a three-day total of 207, nine under par.

The Swede made her mark on the Crooked Stick course at Carmel in the three holes before the turn, when she went **birdie**, birdie, **eagle**. She then dropped a shot at the tenth and came home in one over

The Guardian,
26 July 1993

However, big trouble awaited him at the 14th.

His drive stopped on top of a bunker. Unable to take a proper stance, he tried to chop it on to the fareway, but succeeded only in clipping the top of the ball.

It jumped up and struck his leg, earning him a two-stroke penalty. Then it rolled into the bunker.

He wedged out, knocked a five iron left of the green, chipped on and missed the putt, finishing with a five over par nine

In 1986, he needed a par at the last hole to tie for the Masters, but took a bogey; later that year, Bob Tway holed a bunker shot at the last hole to beat him in the USPGA Championship. In 1987, Norman lost a play-off for the Masters when Larry Mize chipped on from 30 yards

Independent on Sunday,
25 July 1993

Definitions and examples

Sometimes there is so much difficult jargon in a piece of specialist writing, that the writer includes 'A Glossary of Technical Terms'.
A glossary is simply a list of words or phrases with their meanings explained. There is one at the end of this book.

putter a straight iron-headed golf club.

Entries in a **glossary** will usually be quite simple and contain just the *definition*.

putter *(noun)* a straight iron-headed golf club; 'She used her favourite putter in the championships.'

Entries in a **dictionary** will usually contain not only the *definition*, but also the *word class*, and an *example* of how the word might be used.

GETTING TECHNICAL

1 Make up a glossary of technical terms for any activity which you are interested in. This could be anything from cookery to karate!

2 Write an article about your chosen activity, which will help newcomers to understand some of the specialist jargon. You will probably need to use most of the words from your glossary.

LANGUAGE IN USE

Write a helpful leaflet for pupils new to your school, explaining which particular slang expressions and jargon terms are in use.
You may wish to divide it up into two sections, Slang and Jargon.

Section 1: Slang
Introduction – 'Why we use slang': you could include some of the points that people made in the earlier discussion.
Rest of Slang section: you could explain some of the school slang that you discussed on page 27.
Useful headings might be 'In the Classroom'; 'In the Playground'.
You might write some conversations to illustrate this.

Section 2: Jargon
Specialist jargon: you could include some jargon used in particular subjects, e.g. science or technology, or the titles given to certain staff.
Conclusion: Include a Glossary of the terms that you have used.

WRITING AND AUDIENCE

Play Reading

The Granny Project, featured in this unit, is a play about a group of children faced with a problem. You are going to rehearse this short scene, which is the opening of the play, in groups of seven. First decide who is going to play which part.

This is how the characters are described in the cast list:

The Characters

Ivan: Fourteen, serious, and uncompromising. He is in the same school class as his sister –

Sophie: Nearly a year younger, and the brains of the family.

Tanya: Ten, sharp-tongued and impatient. She takes her frustration at being younger than Ivan and Sophie out on –

Nicholas: Nine. Solemn and innocent; a bit of a day-dreamer.

Henry Harris: The children's father. Forty-two, tired, balding and occasionally dispirited. He teaches languages at the school Ivan and Sophie attend. He is married to –

Natasha Harris: The children's mother. Thirty-six, she is Russian by birth and upbringing, and fiery and tense by nature. She can never work out quite how she ended up trapped in a 'foreign' city suburb with four 'foreign' children and an old lady to care for.

The Doctor: Young and inexperienced. He takes refuge in long medical words.

Read the scene through to get an idea of what it is about.
Then read it again, acting out the parts as effectively as you can.
You might record your second reading and compare it with the one on the cassette.

The Granny Project

Act 1

*(The play takes place in a large, untidy family kitchen and living area.
On one side, stools surround a table in front of the oven, sink and fridge.
On the other, two tatty armchairs and a few floor cushions are grouped around
a television. There are several doors off. The table is set for four, with sausages
and mashed potatoes already cooling on the plates.*
Nicholas *comes in, eyeing one of the closed doors uneasily. He hushes
the audience chatter with a damping down gesture of two spread hands.)*

Nicholas: Sssh. Sssh! You'll have to be quiet, all of you. It's very important. My gran's in there, behind that door, and she needs absolute quiet. She's busy. She's dying. For all I know, she

could be dead already. (He *takes a plastic toy soldier off the table and starts twisting its arms and legs around nervously.*) It's been going on for a week now, her dying. Everyone's worn out. Mum and Dad especially. They've been taking turns to sit up with her every night since Monday. Dad's got huge bags under his eyes. Mum looks grey. (He *puts the toy down and faces the audience squarely.*) It's all my brother Ivan's fault. Well, Tanya – she's my sister – she says it's all his fault. But Tanya's always saying spiteful things. Sophie – she's my other sister – she tries to shut Tanya up, but… oh, this is hopeless. This is no way to explain. I'll have to go right back to the beginning and tell you how it happened from the very start, weeks and weeks ago, the day the doctor first came round to our house to fill in the forms.

(**Henry**, **Natasha**, **Ivan**, **Sophie**, **Tanya**, *and the* **Doctor** *come in. The children take their places at the table and start eating silently but very fast.* **Henry** *hunches gloomily on one of the chairs.* **Natasha** *leans against a door with a comtemptuous look on her face. The* **Doctor** *sits upright, filling in his long form.*)

Nicholas:	(*Taking his place at the table*) There we all were, minding our own business, politely eating our supper.
	(**Ivan** *suddenly spins a sausage off his plate onto the floor and reaches down with a fork to stab it.*)
Natasha:	No need to kill your food. It's already dead.
	(**Ivan** *spits a little out onto the side of his plate.*)
Natasha:	Nor is it poisoned! And so you needn't spit it on the plate.
Ivan:	That's gristle, that is!
Natasha:	Tsssk!

Doctor:	(*Filling in the form*) Osteoarthritis. Metacarpophalangeal joint involvement leading to characteristic volar subluxation and ulnar deviation of the phalanges…
Henry:	What?
Sophie:	He says Granny's fingers are bent.
Henry:	Ah.
Doctor:	Degenerative changes in the cochlea…
Sophie:	And she's going deaf.
Henry:	Right.
Doctor:	Impairment of brain tissue function with concomitant deterioration of cognitive functioning…
Natasha:	And stupid, too.
Henry:	Natasha!
Natasha:	Tssk!
Sophie:	She's still smart enough to get to the newspaper every morning before anyone else.
Natasha:	What's in a newspaper to interest you?
Sophie:	Stuff. Stuff for Projects. Any old stuff.
Ivan:	Everything interests me and Sophie now we do Social Science – Crime, Violence, Police Corruption, Race Relations, Consumer Protection, Suicide Rates, Sex, Statistics…
Natasha:	Tssk! Projects! Pah! Such a school. For all your father teaches there, I'll take you out of it! Projects!
Doctor:	There's no specific ambulatory problem, I take it.
Natasha:	The lazy old woman can still walk, yes, if she is truly hungry.
Sophie:	More of a shuffle, really.
Henry:	Well, that's because she stole my bedroom slippers. They're several sizes too large for her feet.
Doctor:	Her dietary intake?
Natasha:	That woman can eat anything!
Ivan:	She ate the leaves off Sophie's geranium last week. And Nicholas and Tanya caught her chewing feathers this morning.
Natasha:	You did? How many?
Nicholas:	Hardly any.
Tanya:	Tons and tons.
Natasha:	See! Stupid and greedy, that is what she is!
Henry:	Natasha! Please!
Natasha:	(*Muttering*) And she should know the cost of pillows.
Henry:	Ssssh.
Natasha:	Tsssk, yourself, Henry Harris! She is not my mother!
Doctor:	(*Folding up the form and rising*) One further manifestation, should we see it, of the proven versatility of the human gastro-intestinal tract.
Natasha:	Just what I said. The woman can eat anything.

Doctor: I'll see these forms get to the right place. But since there's no immediate problem (**Natasha** *glares at him horribly*) Since Mrs Harris isn't actually ill at the moment, results may not be immediate.

Ivan: What does he mean? Results? What's going on? Are you two thinking of putting Granny in a Home?

Natasha: Thinking is finished. It is decided.

Ivan: Dad? Dad?

Henry: (*Clearing his throat in an embarrassed fashion*) Your mother and I are finding Granny an enormous strain…

Nicholas: You're never sending Granny away?

Henry: Nothing's decided. Nothing for you to worry about. Let's wait and see.

Natasha: (*Ushering out the* **Doctor**) Шило в мешке не утаишь.

[Shilo vmiéskay nye ootáish]

Ivan: What?

Sophie: What did she say?

Tanya: What was that?

Nicholas: What did she just say?

Henry: Nothing.

Children: Dad!

Henry: It's only one of her old Russian proverbs.

Sophie: We know that, Dad. But what does it mean?

Henry: It means… (*He hangs his head in shame*) …It means you can't hide sharp steel spikes in soft cloth bags.

(**Henry** *goes out after the* **Doctor** *and* **Natasha**.)

Sophie: (*Sarcastically*) Terrific.

Tanya: Lovely.

Ivan: Really caring.

Nicholas: I think it's horrible. Horrible.

(*A pause. They are all sunk in thought. Then* **Ivan** *claps his hands.*)

Ivan: Meeting! Meeting! Fall in. Take your places.

(*They quickly form a practised semicircle, and sit down.*)

Ivan: Ready?

All: Ready.

Ivan: Good. Right. First thing. Do we care?

All: Yes, we do.

Ivan: Good. Right. Next thing. Can we stop them?

All: Yes we can.

Ivan: Good. Right. Last thing. How?

(*Silence*)

Tanya: I could have some of my tantrums. Or my nightmares. My tantrums and nightmares really get on their nerves.

Nicholas: They really get on mine as well. I vote against that.

Ivan:	How about a strike? No fetching in the coal, no washing-up, no going down to the shops, till they back down.
Nicholas:	They're tougher than we are. They practically remember the war. We'll freeze and starve and live in even more of a mess than we do now, and they'll still win. I vote against that.
Ivan:	Do you have any brilliant ideas of your own?
Nicholas:	Send them to Coventry. Don't say a word to either until they change their minds.
Ivan:	You must be mad. They'd simply be grateful for all the peace and quiet. They've often said as much. Sophie, you're supposed to be the brains here. Sophie?
	(**Sophie** *is sunk in thought. Light dawns and she lifts her head.*)
Sophie:	I've got it!

Anne Fine

WHAT HAPPENS NEXT?

In your groups discuss:
● what you might do if you were in the children's position
● what you think Sophie's idea might be. (A clue is in the play's title.)

Turn to page 90 to find out what the children actually decide to do.

In a well-written play we can see what the characters are like by the language they use.

In the same groups, decide what the dialogue tells us about the Doctor and Natasha. Pick out three speeches of the Doctor's and three of Natasha's in which the language shows most clearly what the characters are like. In the Doctor's case you may want to look back at page 31 in Unit 3 on jargon.

What is a playscript?

In Book 1, Unit 4 you learned about topic, form, audience, and purpose. What happens if we look at these in relation to a playscript?

THE TOPIC AND THE FORM

1   Plays, like poems and novels, can be about anything. From these opening pages, what would you say the topic of *The Granny Project* was?

2   In pairs, look back at the extract you have just read. List all the things which show that it is from a playscript (rather than from a novel). When you have completed your list, compare it with the notes on page 68 in Book 1.

3   Look again at the cast list. What kinds of information does the playwright provide about the characters here? How useful do you find it?

THE AUDIENCE AND THE PURPOSE

Any playscript will have more than one possible audience. Its readers will include the people who:
- are intending to act the play
- are going to direct it and do all the 'backstage' work
- simply want to read it

1   Who are the main audience for *The Granny Project* in this book? (Note that, when we use the term 'audience' in this way, it means something slightly different from the audience who will finally sit down to watch a performance of the play itself.)

2   One purpose of a playscript is always likely to be 'to entertain'. But, having read the opening of *The Granny Project*, can you think of any other purposes that the playwright might have had?

Stage Directions

If you were showing this to a younger reader who had never seen a play before, how would you explain why some of the writing was in italics?

The sections in italics are known as **stage directions**.

We have already looked at these in Book 1, Unit 7 but here are some more detailed points about them.

Stage directions and characters

Some stage directions are simply short phrases helping us to understand what the character is supposed to be doing:

e.g. **Nicholas:** (*Taking his place at the table*)

Sometimes they show how a line should be said:

e.g. **Natasha:** (*Muttering*)

Find other examples in the extract of brief stage directions used in these ways.

Stage directions and the 'set'

At the beginning of the play there is a longer section of stage directions which describes the **set** – the setting (furniture, walls, etc) in which the actors act.

Reread the opening stage directions (from 'The play takes place…' to 'cooling on the plates' on page 34). Then draw either a picture or a plan of the set based on the description.

When you have completed your picture or plan, compare it with a partner's and discuss any differences.

Go to the Drama section of your library and find other plays with interesting descriptions of the set. You could make a display of these with plans or illustrations to go with them.

Stage directions and tenses

Stage directions are always written in the *present tense* (as though things were happening now rather than in the *past*).

e.g. The play *takes place*…(rather than …*took place*).

You can remind yourself about verb tenses by looking back at Book 1, page 78.

Look through the stage directions, from the point where Henry says 'It means…' on page 37 to the end, and pick out the other verbs in the present tense. Check your list with the one on page 90.

Here is an illustration of the set for *Sherlock Holmes and the Limehouse Horror* by Philip Pullman.

1   Write the stage directions which describe the set, as they might appear at the beginning of a script. Remember that stage directions are for people, such as actors and others organizing the play, who do not have a plan or illustration. Your directions therefore need to be extremely clear.

2   Imagine that one of your favourite novels is to be turned into a play. Draw the set for any one scene and then write the stage directions based on your drawing.
    If you were to choose *My Mate Shofiq*, you might describe the Head's office. The passage on pages 16-17 would help you to decide what furniture was needed on the set, but you would have to use your imagination to add all the other details.

Stage speak

Left and right...

In the picture, there is a slipper to the left of the set as we are looking at it. But when we write stage directions, we say that the slipper is 'to the right' of the set, because that is how the actors on stage would see it. Sometimes stage directions will talk about a slipper being **stage right**...

...and up and down

Many stages have a slope (known as a 'rake') so that the actors at the back can be seen more easily. Because of this we talk about things being **upstage** if they are at the back and **downstage** if they are at the front. There is also a mid-stage area called **centre stage**.

Giving Information in Dialogue

If you are writing a short story or a novel, you can easily give the reader all sorts of information in the narrative, as indeed Anne Fine did when she originally wrote *The Granny Project* as a novel. But in a playscript you cannot write pages and pages of stage directions, so most of this information has to come through the dialogue.

Shakespeare's opening scenes

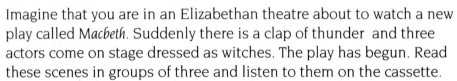

Imagine that you are in an Elizabethan theatre about to watch a new play called *Macbeth*. Suddenly there is a clap of thunder and three actors come on stage dressed as witches. The play has begun. Read these scenes in groups of three and listen to them on the cassette.

Macbeth

Act 1 Scene 1   (*On the moor*)

(*Thunder and lightning. Enter three* **Witches**.)

First Witch:
When shall we three meet again
In thunder, lightning, or in rain?
Second Witch:
When the hurlyburly's done,
When the battle's lost and won.
Third Witch:
5   That will be ere the set of sun.
First Witch:
Where the place?
Second Witch: Upon the heath.
Third Witch:
There to meet with Macbeth.
First Witch:
I come, Graymalkin! [1]
Second Witch:
             Paddock[1] calls.
10   **Third Witch:**   Anon.[2]
All:
Fair is foul, and foul is fair:
Hover through the fog and filthy air.   (*Exeunt*)

Scene 2   (*A camp near Forres*)

(*Alarum. Enter* **King Duncan**, **Malcolm**, **Donalbain**, **Lennox**, *with* **Attendants**, *meeting a bleeding* **Sergeant**.)
Duncan:
What bloody man is that? He can report,

[1] *Greymalkin* and *Paddock* are probably the Witches' evil spirit attendants.

[2] *Anon* means 'immediately'.

As seemeth by his plight, of the revolt
The newest state.

    Malcolm: This is the sergeant
Who, like a good and hardy soldier, fought
5   'Gainst my captivity. Hail, brave friend!
Say to the king the knowledge of the broil
As thou didst leave it.

    Sergeant: Doubtful it stood;
As two spent swimmers, that do cling together
And choke their art.¹ The merciless Macdonwald –
10   Worthy to be a rebel, for to that
The muliplying villainies of nature
Do swarm upon him – from the western isles
Of kerns and gallowglasses² is supplied;
And fortune, on his damned quarrel smiling,
15   Show'd like a rebel's whore: but all's too weak;
For brave Macbeth – well he deserves that name –
Disdaining fortune, with his brandish'd steel
Which smok'd with bloody execution,
Like valour's minion carv'd out his passage
20   Till he fac'd the slave;
Which ne'er shook hands, nor bade farewell to him,
Till he unseam'd him from the nave to the chaps,³
And fix'd his head upon our battlements.

William Shakespeare

¹ …*choke their art* means 'make the art
of swimming impossible'.

² *Kerns and gallowglasses* are types of Celtic
soldier from the Hebrides ('the Western Isles').

³ …*from the nave to the chaps* means 'from
the navel to the jaws' (or 'chops').

LISTENING FOR INFORMATION

In the same groups list what we learn from
these opening scenes about:
- the characters. Who are they? Where have
  they come from? How do they feel about
  things? What are their plans?
- the story. What has happened so far?
  What might happen next?
- the setting. Where is the action taking
  place? What do we imagine it to be like?

PREDICTING FROM THE INFORMATION

1   From the things the Witches say and the
language they use (e.g. 'Fair is foul and
foul is fair...') discuss what kinds of things
we expect to happen in this play.

2   To show how much information the
audience learns from the first part of Act 1
Scene 2, write a short newspaper article
with this headline:
REBELS DEFEATED AT FORRES
You might begin it something like this:

In one of the bloodiest battles ever fought
on Scottish soil, Macdonwald and his rebel
army were finally defeated at Forres today, writes
Special Correspondent…

Speaking to the Audience

In the opening of *The Granny Project* Nicholas speaks directly to the audience. Although he is a character, he is suddenly part of the audience too and they become part of the play.

1   Write down the information that Nicholas provides in this speech which would be particularly difficult to get across through dialogue with other characters.

2   What other purposes does Nicholas' speech have, apart from giving information? Can you find a point at which he is expressing opinions, for example?

3   In your library look at the openings to these other plays:
Romeo and Juliet by William Shakespeare
Across the Barricades by Joan Lingard (playscript by David Ian Neville)
Billy Liar by Keith Waterhouse and Willis Hall
In each opening a character speaks directly to the audience. For each play decide:
● what information is provided by this speech to the audience
● whether the audience really needs this information
● whether it could have been conveyed through dialogue
● what purposes the speech has in addition to giving information

LANGUAGE IN USE

1   Try writing the opening of your own play. Before you start to write and as you plan it out, think about these key points.

The topic
What might your play be about? Anne Fine's is her adaptation of her own novel. If you have a favourite novel, you might like to try turning part of that into the opening of a play.

Try to include a central 'conflict', as *The Granny Project* does. This could come out of some incident at home or in school. Alternatively, you might base the story in a Science Fiction or Fantasy World. The illustrations on this page might offer some ideas for characters and settings if you get stuck.

The form

Think about the following possible 'ingredients' which are important for the playscript form.

Character list: when you have decided on your characters (six or seven at most) draw up a cast list with information about characters similar to that provided for *The Granny Project* on page 34.

Description of the set: set your play in a room or other setting which can be described clearly in your first stage directions. Remember that they are always written in the present tense.

Short stage directions in the dialogue: these are helpful in explaining what actions are going on or how the characers are saying things.

The dialogue: this needs to contain all the useful information about characters, the story or the setting (if that is not obvious from the set). You might choose to have one of your characters speaking direct to the audience, if that is the best way to get certain information across.

Layout: refer back to page 68 of Book 1 to remind yourself how playscripts are set out.

2   When you have completed your scene, rehearse and perform it with some friends. You could record it on cassette, so that you can talk about any changes which might be made. Then discuss what might happen in the rest of your play.

Words and Memories

Whenever we come to write a poem the most important tools that we possess are our memories and our imaginations.
Read this poem by Seamus Heaney in which he recalls times from his childhood in Ireland at the seaside village of Inishbofin.

Inishbofin

Inishbofin on a Sunday morning.
Sunlight, turfsmoke, seagulls, boatslip, diesel.
One by one we were being handed down
Into a boat that dipped and shilly-shallied
Scaresomely every time. We sat tight
On short cross-benches, in nervous twos and threes,
Obedient, newly close, nobody speaking
Except the boatmen, as the gunwales sank
And seemed they might ship water any minute.
The sea was very calm but even so,
When the engine kicked and our ferryman
Swayed for balance, reaching for the tiller,
I panicked at the shiftiness and heft
Of the craft itself. What guaranteed us –
That quick response and buoyancy and swim –
Kept me in agony. All the time
As we went sailing evenly across
The deep, still, seeable-down-into water,
It was as if I looked from another boat
Sailing through air, far up, and could see
How riskily we fared into the morning,
And loved in vain our bare, bowed, numbered heads.

Seamus Heaney

USING MEMORIES

1 With a partner, pick out the phrases which you think best describe the poet's feelings about the boat trip.

 2 Listen again to the poem, this time as it is read on the cassette. Then talk about any childhood memories you have that are similar to this one. Which senses in particular help you to recall scenes like this: sight, hearing, touch, smell or taste?

POETRY AND NOUNS

Many poets say that the most important words in a memory poem are the *nouns*, the 'names' or 'labels' of the places, people or things that the poet wants to recall and write about. If you need to remind yourself about nouns, turn back to pages 74-75 of The Reference Section in Book 1.

Look back at the poem and discuss the following questions in pairs.

1 How many of the ten words which make up the opening two lines are nouns?

2 Nearly all the nouns in the poem are common nouns, but *Inishbofin* and *Sunday* are proper nouns – the name of a particular place and a particular time. What difference does it make to have proper nouns rather than common nouns right at the beginning of the poem?

3 Which other nouns – there are at least ten – have something to do with boats? How many of these would you use in everyday conversation and how many of them are more 'specialist' words? Does it make the poem more interesting to have specialist words, such as 'gunwales', or do you find it off-putting?

POETRY AND THE SENSES

Not all of our memories are to do with things that we have seen. Often we remember smells, tastes, sounds and the way things felt to the touch.

On your own, look at the five nouns in the second line of *Inishbofin*. When he lists these nouns, Heaney is certainly recalling what the scene *looked* like; but each of these words may have an effect on our other senses too. Which senses of yours are triggered by each of these nouns? It will be different for different people.

Your Own Memories

Many poems are about ordinary events which are for some reason special to the poet. Heaney based his poem on a simple childhood memory of being frightened in a small boat at the seaside.

'Finding a stray dog'.

'Being in the Nativity play'.

'Our garden in autumn.'
Burning leaves on the bonfire.
Clipping the hedge.
Wasps around the apples.

Remembering

Spend a few minutes thinking back to when you were a child – or perhaps the more recent past. Jot down any memories of a scene or an event which sticks in your mind. You might use some of the ideas you came up with on page 47. Remember that it can be something extremely ordinary; but it does need to be important to you.

Listing

Now make a list of all the nouns which have something to do with your particular memory. These might be the names of all the objects, people, animals or places which come to mind when you think about your chosen scene or event. One or two might be proper nouns: the name of a particular place or person.

'Our garden in autumn'
apples
leaves
smoke
ash
corn
wasps
combine harvester...

Sensing

As we have seen, Seamus Heaney's nouns made us use several of our senses. We might have smelt the turfsmoke, felt the sunlight and heard the seagulls, as well as seeing all of them.

Go through your list of nouns and see how many senses are involved. Rearrange your list under five headings like this, so that there is at least one noun for each of the senses. Some nouns might end up under more than one heading.

Taste: air smoke ash
Sound: shears leaves wind
        wasps harvester bee
Smell: apples corn smoke air
Touch: leaves night-air
Sight: smoke ash leaves
        wasps harvester bee
        apples corn shears

Bringing it all together

This is how thirteen-year-old Ruth Kingshott used her own vivid sense memories of her garden in autumn in order to write a poem called *Senses*. You will find a reading of the poem on the cassette.

Senses

Taste
The dry, musty leaves
Which tamper with the air,
Lingering smoke,
The taste of ash.

Hear
The clip of the shears
As they prune the hedge.
Listen to the leaves
As they throw a tantrum
In the wind.

Smell
The sweet fragrance
From soft brown apples
Feasted by wasps,
The dusty corn
Thrown from the yellow harvester.

See
The rust colour
Painted through the garden.
See the bee,
Flying,
Weighed down by boots of yellow
    pollen.

Touch
The leaves
Crumbling with dryness.
Feel the bitter night
In the air
Of my autumn garden.

Ruth Kingshott

WRITING YOUR OWN: THE FIRST DRAFT

Use your notes to write the first draft of a sense poem of your own. You already have a collection of important nouns arranged according to the senses they are connected with.

You might now find it helpful to follow the pattern of Ruth Kingshott's poem and have five short sections, each in turn beginning with the invitation to taste, hear, smell, see, and touch…

Ruth's poem happens to be based upon a garden near a cornfield, but you are writing about what you know and remember.

Finally, remember that this is no more than a first draft. When you have completed it, put your draft to one side to be worked on later.

Sounds and Images

Poetry is not only about the particular words which our memories provide for us when we want to write about a scene or event from the past.

When we write a poem there are at least three other important things we have to think about:

- the pictures that we create to help the reader
- the kinds of sentences we need to use and the order of the words
- the sounds of the words and phrases

Think about those things as you read these three poems. You might need to read each one silently at first and then aloud. When you have read them, discuss in pairs the questions that follow. Each of the poems is also read on the cassette.

The Eagle

He clasps the crag with crooked hands;
Close to the sun in lonely lands,
Ring'd with the azure world he stands.

The wrinkled sea beneath him crawls;
He watches from his mountain walls,
And like a thunderbolt he falls.

Alfred Lord Tennyson

Pigeons

They paddle with staccato feet
In powder-pools of sunlight,
Small blue busybodies
Strutting like fat gentlemen
With hands clasped
Under their swallowtail coats;
And, as they stump about,
Their heads like tiny hammers
Tap at imaginary nails
In non-existent walls.
Elusive ghosts of sunshine
Slither down the green gloss
Of their necks an instant, and are gone.

Summer hangs drugged from sky to earth
In limpid fathoms of silence:
Only warm dark dimples of sound
Slide like slow bubbles
From the contented throats.

Raise a casual hand –
With one quick gust
They fountain into air.

Richard Kell

Grey Owl

When fireflies begin to wink
over the stubble near the wood,
ghost-of-the-air,
the grey owl, glides into dusk

Over the spruce, a drift of smoke,
over the juniper knoll,
whispering wings
making the sound of silk unfurling,
in the soft blur of starlight
a puff of feathers blown about.

Terrible fixed eyes,
talons sheathed in down,
refute this floating wraith.

Before the shapes of mist
show white beneath the moon,
the rabbit or the rat
will know the knives of fire,
the pothooks swinging out of space.

But now the muffled hunter
moves like smoke, like wind,
scarcely apprehended,
barely glimpsed and gone,
like a grey thought
fanning the margins of the mind.

Joseph Payne Brennan

LOOKING CLOSELY AT THE POEMS

1   Which qualities of *The Eagle* come across
    most clearly to you? List some abstract
    nouns (e.g. pride, loneliness) which
    seem to fit the picture that you have
    formed in your mind.

2   If you were making a thirty-second film to
    accompany a reading of *Pigeons*, which
    seven or eight shots would you choose?

3   Prepare a reading of *Grey Owl*.
    You might wish to use some of the
    reading techniques suggested on pages
    22-23 in Book 1, Unit 2.

Pictures in Poetry

Comparing images

Whenever we explain something, describe a scene or tell a story, we find ourselves quite naturally wanting to make comparisons. We say *It was like…* or *I felt as if…*
Sometimes we cut out the 'like' and say, *She ploughed through her work*, (comparing her effort to the action of a plough) or *The sun smiled down on us* (comparing the sun to a person).
Three of the different kinds of comparison that we make, are known as simile, metaphor, and personification.

SIMILES IN POETRY

When the poet Tennyson wants to describe the way in which the eagle falls from the crag, he uses a comparison:
'…and *like a thunderbolt* he falls.'
We can imagine the speed, power and danger of a thunderbolt and this helps us to picture how the eagle dives.

This kind of comparison, in which a writer says that something is like or as something else, is called a **simile**. For a simile to be really effective, the poet has to find a comparison with something unusual or unexpected.

1 Find and discuss the similes in *Pigeons*. How successfully does the first one help us to imagine the way the birds walk, the second one the movement of their heads, and the third the way the sounds come from their throats?

2 Joseph Payne Brennan describes the grey owl moving 'like smoke, like wind… like a grey thought' Invent similes to describe:
● a bird standing on one leg in water
● the sound of the cuckoo
● a sparrow having a bath in a puddle
● a duck walking
● a kestrel hovering

If we wanted to invent a simile to describe how a flock of pigeons suddenly take off, we might write:

> They fly up into the air like a fountain.

Instead Richard Kell writes:

> They fountain into air.

This kind of comparison – in which the writer makes a comparison but does not actually 'spell it out' – is called a **metaphor**.

1   Find the metaphor that Ruth Kingshott uses to describe the bees' pollen sacs?

2   Which metaphor in P*igeons* describes the effect of sunlight on the birds' neck feathers? What is being compared with what, exactly?

PERSONIFICATION

There is a special kind of metaphor, in which an animal, object or thing is described as though it were a person and had the same kinds of thoughts, actions or attitudes that a human being might have. For example, the leaves in the poem S*enses* 'tamper' with the air and 'throw a tantrum' in the wind, as though they were mischievous and bad-tempered people. This is called **personification**.

1   What kind of people do we imagine the pigeons to be in Richard Kell's poem?

2   Look up the expression 'shilly-shally' in your dictionary and then find it in I*nishbofin*, the poem on page 46. How does this personification help us to understand what the boat is doing?

Poetry, Sentences, and Word Order

Sentences in poetry

The bird poems – as well as the ones by Seamus Heaney and Ruth Kingshott – show that you can do things quite naturally with sentences in poetry which are much harder to do with prose.
Prose is the name we give to most of the writing that we produce and read. (Nearly everything we read including short stories, articles or letters will be in prose.)

Sentences in a poem can –
- be very long: e.g. the opening ten lines of *Grey Owl*, which is all one sentence
- have no verb: e.g. the first sentence of *Inishbofin*
- be divided up very regularly: e.g each of the two sentences of *The Eagle*

All of these things are also possible in prose, but are much more common as part of the language of poetry.

LISTENING FOR MEANING

 1 Read *The Eagle* aloud, taking notice of the punctuation. Then listen to the reading on the cassette. What do you notice about the way in which each of the two sentences is divided up? How do those divisions help you to read the poem and understand its meaning?

2 Divide a page into six 'frames' and write a line of *The Eagle* below each. Do a rough sketch of the picture that comes to mind for each line. Then pick the one that most interests you and produce a more careful illustration. The results could form part of a class display.

Word order in poetry

Sometimes a poem has exactly the same word order as it would in prose. However, a poet often gets a more interesting effect by changing the word order. We can also make particular words stand out by placing them at the beginning of a line.

LOOKING FOR EMPHASIS

1 Look back at the five poems in this unit and find examples of:
- three phrases which have an ordinary prose word order, e.g. 'He clasps the crag with crooked hands'
- one phrase in which the word order is different from the usual prose word order, e.g. 'And like a thunderbolt he falls.' (Usually we would say, 'And he falls like a thunderbolt.')

Take your example of unusual word order and say what effect you think this different word order has, like this:

And like a thunderbolt he falls.

(A poem's 'climax' is the most interesting moment that the previous lines build up to. Climax comes from a Greek word meaning 'ladder'.)

2 Reread *Grey Owl* and see how noticeable the words 'ghost' and 'talons' are because they are placed at the beginnings of lines. Then find words in Ruth Kingshott's *Senses* and Seamus Heaney's *Inishbofin* which are noticeable for the same reason.

WRITING YOUR OWN: THE SECOND DRAFT

Return to the first draft of your poem. Look again at these areas.

- *Sentences*: are your sentences all roughly the same length? Can you change any of the line lengths, in order to stress one part of the poem rather than another or to encourage the reader to read a line in a certain way?

- *Word order*: have you used prose word order all the time? Could you change the word order in some cases so as to stress particular phrases or single words?

- *Line beginnings*: are there any lines that you could change, so that important words are placed at the beginning?

Sound Effects in Poetry

In the best poetry the sounds of the words and phrases play a crucial part in helping to make the meaning. A poet does not put words together simply because they 'sound interesting'.

The most common 'sound effects' which are used to get the meaning across are *alliteration*, *onomatopoeia*, and *rhyme*. (You have already met the first two in Book 1, Unit 2.)

GETTING THE EFFECT

It is easy to 'spot' alliteration or onomatopoeia in a poem, but sometimes difficult to say what their *effects* are. Often they simply draw attention to certain words or phrases or help to underline a meaning.

1   Find examples of alliteration in *Grey Owl* and try to say what their effect is.

2   To get the effect of the onomatopoeia in *Grey Owl*, read lines 7 to 10 in a whisper:

   'whispering wings…'

   How does the onomatopoeia help us to understand the meaning of this phrase?

3   Find the onomatopoeic lines in *Pigeons*. In your opinion do they successfully echo the sound that the birds make? How important is the onomatopoeia in helping us to understand the description?

Rhyme

Why do some poems rhyme and others not? Some poets feel that regular rhyme helps the reader to 'tick off' each section of the poem, as complete.

From the five poems in this unit, only *The Eagle* has a regular **rhyme scheme** or rhyming pattern.

Many poets would advise you to avoid rhyme unless you had a special reason for using it.

What special effect does the rhyme have in *The Eagle*? (Notice that there are three rhyming words in each group.)

Rhyme and meaning

The Eagle is unusual because it could make sense if the lines were in a different order.

Working in pairs, one of you write out the poem on a piece of paper. Then cut out each of the lines separately and rearrange them so that they still make sense.

What is the new rhyme scheme? How do the new line order and new rhyme scheme change the meanings?

LANGUAGE IN USE

Write the final drafts of your *Senses* poem.

It would be quite wrong to suggest that you had to use examples of simile, metaphor and personification; or that your poem had to rhyme and include onomatopoeia and alliteration. But at least you will now be aware that all of these are part of the language of poetry and some may well find their way into your poem. But they should only be there if they help the meaning.

Using Encyclopedias

What do you know about the early form of writing pictured below?

1   In pairs, look at the photograph and try to decide what kind of substance the writing is made on and what sort of tool the writer used. (Looking at the shape of the strokes made will help you to work this out.)

2   How might you find out more about this early form of writing?
    You could certainly ask teachers or a librarian. But they are most likely to suggest that you try to find some good information books.

First stop – the encyclopedia

Encyclopedias are the easiest reference books to use, because their entries are in alphabetical order. For example, if we look up the subject 'Writing' in the *Oxford Children's Encyclopedia*, we find an entry which contains some of the information we want.

1   With your partner, read this encyclopedia article about 'Writing Systems' and then discuss these questions.
    ● Which facts about writing did you find most interesting?
    ● What other things did you learn, which were totally new to you?
    ● What can you now say about the first example of early writing that you looked at?

2   Look at the 'See also' section. If you wanted to find out more about the origins of writing, which other articles in this encyclopedia would be most helpful?

3   If your school or local library has this encyclopedia, look up those other entries and write down any further facts they provide about writing. Save this information for 'Language in use' on page 67.

Writing Systems

We send language messages in two quite different ways: we say them or we write them. We write ideas or words down when we want either to keep them and remember them later, or to let someone else read them at a later time or in a different place. Writing is a way of recording and sorting words and ideas. Famous books, the country's laws, scientific discoveries, letters to friends: these are all written down, to be read or remembered for various purposes later.

Before writing

Many early peoples kept an 'oral' record of the great events of their history or beliefs. This means that some people learnt the record by heart (perhaps in a long poem) and recited it to others in their society. The poem about the great war between the Greeks and Trojans called the *Iliad* is an example of this. It was recited for a long time before it was finally written down.

Pictograms and ideograms

Pictograms are an early form of communication. Pictures of objects, such as a circle for the Sun, represented the object itself. In ideograms the whole idea of the word is explained in a shape rather like a picture. The Chinese and Japanese use ideograms instead of using an alphabet.

Early writing systems

The earliest true writing was developed by the Sumerians in the land of Mesopotamia (now Iraq). The earliest examples found come from Tell Brak and are dated to about 3250 BC. The language was discovered on a very large number (over 250,000) of clay tablets. They used wedge-shaped signs on the tablets to develop a type of writing know as cuneiform. Cuneiform was used for about 3,000 years.

From about 3100 BC the ancient Egyptians developed a different form of writing called heiroglyphics. Their writing system used pictures at first, but the pictures did not enable them to explain complicated ideas. They developed a system which used picture signs to represent sounds. The Egyptians carved and painted these heiroglyphs on stone, but they also wrote with rush pens on papyrus, a sort of paper made from crushed reeds.

The first proper alphabet to be used was developed in Syria in the 15th century BC.

◀ **Chinese ideograms. The earliest forms were simple but recognizable drawings. Over the centuries they changed into stylized shapes that are easy to write.**

We use signs for mathematical ideas such as + = - x, and for money: £ and $. These are similar to ideograms.

See also

Alphabets
Braille
Calligraphy
Communication
Heiroglyphics
Sumerians

Oxford Children's Encyclopedia

Where else can you look?

As well as many different encyclopedias, there are hundreds of information or reference books in most libraries. Reference books can often give you more information than an encyclopedia entry; but it is sometimes difficult to know which ones will give you the information you need.

Using Information Books

If you visit your local library and ask where you might find information on 'writing in ancient civilizations', a helpful librarian will point you towards the right shelf. But how do you know whether a particular book is going to be useful or not?
There are two things that you can do.

Step 1: Checking the Contents page

Many people look quickly at the **Contents page** of an information book, to see whether it appears to contain the kind of information that they are looking for.
A Contents page lists the titles of the book's chapters or sections and the order in which they appear.

A

Ancient Egyptians,
Fiona Macdonald

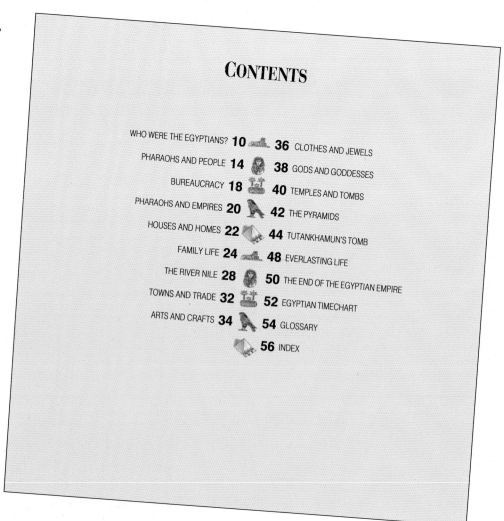

1 Look carefully at these three Contents pages.

2 Decide in each case which book:
- will probably have information about only one writing system
- will probably tell you about a wide variety of writing systems (because it is totally about writing and nothing else)
- is likely to contain several short references to writing, spread around sections on many different topics
- seems to be extremely 'technical' (pick out examples of the language which tell you this)

3 Look at the contents of books B and C. List the sections or pages which you might look up if you were trying to find information about
- ancient Chinese writing
- early writing in the American continent (before Europeans first visited)

The Usborne's Children's World History, J. Tyler, L. Watts, and R. Gee

4 From its Contents page, how much information about early writing do you expect to find in book A? (You will find the answer on pages 62-63.)

B

Contents

A History of Writing, A. Gaur

C

Contents

Step 2: Checking the Index

Book A, *Ancient Egyptians*, does, in fact, contain a great deal of information about writing, though you might not have been able tell that by looking at its Contents page. To find out exactly what is in a book, you have to turn to a different part altogether.

An **Index** gives you much more detailed information than a Contents page. It will have a list, in alphabetical order, of all the subjects covered in the book, the names of people and places mentioned, and many of the details referred to in the chapters. (These are known as the **references**.)

A good index allows you to see where particular subjects are dealt with, even though they might occur on odd pages in several different chapters or sections.

Here is the Index from *Ancient Egyptians*.

An index tells you where to look if you want to find a particular subject.

References can be to particular places or people or more general subjects.

An index is always in alphabetical order, like a dictionary.

Page numbers in italics show you where you will find an illustration.

INDEX

(Page numbers in *italics* refer to illustrations and captions.)

A
Abu Simbel *11*, 12
Abydos *11*
acrobats 17
Afghanistan 32
agriculture 10, 25, 26, 35
air-conditioning 17
Akenhaten (pharaoh) 15, *17*, 32, 34
Akhetaten, *see* el-Amarna
Alexander the Great 51
Amenophis III (pharaoh) 16, 39, 40
Amun (god) 32, *40*
animals
  mummified 49
  pests 23, *27*
  sacred, 32, 34, *38*, *39*, *49*
ankh *12*
Anubis (god) *39*
Apis (god) 34, 38, 49
archaeology in Egypt 12–14, 38, 44–7
artists, 34, 35
Aswan *11*, 12, 28
Augustus, Emperor, of Rome 50

B
basalt *10*
Bastet (goddess) 38, *39*, 49
beer brewing 26
boats, Egyptian 20, *47*
The Book of the Dead 19
bread 25
brick making *17*, 22, 23
bronze casting 34, 35
Bubastis 49

C
canopic jar *48*
Carnavon, Lord 45
Carter, Howard 44–6
cats 31
chariot *21*
Cheops (pharaoh) 47
Cleopatra VII (queen) 50, 51
cloth making *24*, 25
Colossi of Memnon *11*
crafts 34, 35
craftsmen *14*
crocodile 19
crocodile god 39
crowns, royal 15
Cyprus 33

D
Dahshur 43
Dendara, Lake *11*, 41

E
Edfu *11*, *38*, 49
Egypt, Ancient
  geography 10, 11, 18, 20, 33
  history 10, 11, 20, 21, 50, 51
Egypt, Lower *10*, 15
Egypt, Upper *11*, 15
Egyptians, Ancient
  dress 15, 36, 37
  food 16, 25–7
  government 14, 15, 18, 19
  homes 23, 24
  introduction to 10, 11
  religion 14, 18, 32, 38, 39
Egyptology 14
el-Amarna (Akhetaten) *10*, 32, 34
emmer wheat 26
Ethiopia 32

F
Faiyum 39
famine 28
farmers 28–32

G
Giza 10, *11*, 15, *42*, 43
glass making 34
Greece 32
Greeks, The 11, *51*

H
Hathor (goddess) 41, *46*
Hatshepsut (queen) *11*, 16, *40*
Heliopolis 32
Herodotus 13
hieroglyphs 13, *15*, 19
hippopotamus 28
Horus (god) *12*, 32, *38*, 49
house building 22, 23
Hyksos People 20
hypostyle halls 13

I
Imhotep 42
inscriptions in stone 12, 13
inventions, Egyptian
  mud brick 22, 23
  paper 18, 19
  Pyramid building 42, 43
  writing 18, 19
Iraq 11
irrigation 28
Isis (goddess) *11*, 33, *48*
Iyneferti (queen) 12

K
Karnak *11–13*, *40*
Khephren (pharaoh) 43
Khufu (pharaoh) *11*, *42*, 43
knife 26

L
lavatories 17
Lebanese 11
Lebanon 32
Libya 11, 33
Libyan invasion of Egypt 50
life expectancy 24, 54
linen making 24, 33, 36
Luxor *11*, *14*, 23, *39*, 40

M
ma'at 39
make-up 36, 37
massage 17
Memphis *10*, 32–4, 49
Menes (pharaoh) 15
mummy 28, 46–9
'Mummy's curse' 45
myrrh 36, 54

N
natron 33, 48, 55
Nefertiti (queen) *10*, *17*
New Kingdom 17, 20
Nile, River *10*, *11*, 18, 20, 26, 28, 29, 33, 39
nomes 32, 55
Nubia, Kingdom of 18, 20, *32*, 50

56

1 Look carefully at the Index, with a partner, and write down the pages on which you expect to find information about:
- writing
- writing materials
- writing implements
- the people who produced the writing
  (And do not just look under 'W'!)

2 Which are the obvious pages to look up first? Select four, one for each of the areas above.

You will often have to look up several pages to find the particular information you are interested in.

3 Which other *references* might also be worth looking up (because, for example, they might contain illustrations of the writing on buildings or sculptures)?
Check your findings with the list on page 90.

Step 3: Turning to the right sections

If we have followed the advice laid out in the Index, we will turn first to pages 12 and 13, or 18 and 19.

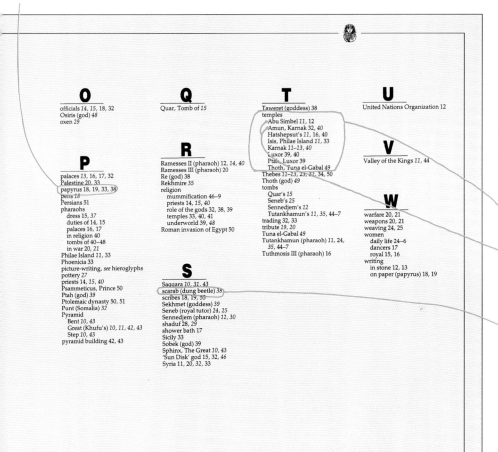

O
officials 14, 15, 18, 32
Osiris (god) 48
oxen 29

P
palaces 13, 16, 17, 32
Palestine 20, 33
papyrus 18, 19, 33, 38
pens 18
Persians 51
pharaohs
  dress 15, 37
  duties of 14, 15
  palaces 16, 17
  in religion 40
  tombs of 40–48
  in war 20, 21
Philae Island 11, 33
Phoenicia 33
picture-writing, *see* hieroglyphs
pottery 27
priests 14, 15, 40
Psammeticus, Prince 50
Ptah (god) 39
Ptolemaic dynasty 50, 51
Punt (Somalia) 32
Pyramid
  Bent 10, 43
  Great (Khufu's) 10, 11, 42, 43
  Step 10, 43
pyramid building 42, 43

Q
Quar, Tomb of 15

R
Ramesses II (pharaoh) 12, 14, 40
Ramesses III (pharaoh) 20
Re (god) 38
Rekhmire 35
religion
  mummification 46–9
  priests 14, 15, 40
  role of the gods 32, 38, 39
  temples 33, 40, 41
  underworld 39, 48
Roman invasion of Egypt 50

S
Saqqara 10, 31, 43
scarab (dung beetle) 38
scribes 18, 19, 35
Sekhmet (goddess) 39
Seneb (royal tutor) 24, 25
Sennedjem (pharaoh) 12, 30
shaduf 28, 29
shower bath 17
Sicily 33
Sobek (god) 39
Sphinx, The Great 10, 43
'Sun Disk' god 15, 32, 46
Syria 11, 20, 32, 33

T
Taweret (goddess) 38
temples
  Abu Simbel 11, 12
  Amun, Karnak 32, 40
  Hatshepsut's 11, 16, 40
  Isis, Philae Island 11, 33
  Karnak 11–13, 40
  Luxor 39, 40
  Ptah, Luxor 39
  Thoth, Tuna el-Gabal 49
Thebes 11–13, 23, 32, 34, 50
Thoth (god) 49
tombs
  Quar's 15
  Seneb's 25
  Sennedjem's 12
  Tutankhamun's 11, 35, 44–7
trading 32, 33
tribute 19, 20
Tuna el-Gabal 49
Tutankhamun (pharaoh) 11, 24, 35, 44–7
Tuthmosis III (pharaoh) 16

U
United Nations Organization 12

V
Valley of the Kings 11, 44

W
warfare 20, 21
weapons 20, 21
weaving 24, 25
women
  daily life 24–6
  dancers 17
  royal 15, 16
writing
  in stone 12, 13
  on paper (papyrus) 18, 19

Some major subjects will be referred to throughout the book. Sub-headings help you to find exactly the details you want.

Unusual specialist words are sometimes explained.

— 57 —

These are pages 18 and 19 from *Ancient Egyptians*. This 'spread' or double page is actually in five sections. Around the main article are three boxes and a photograph with a caption.

Step 4: Reading the main text

The main text first shows how writing became important to the Egyptians and then goes on to describe what that writing was like. Because it tells a 'story', we can draw up a plan of it which shows how one point leads on to another.

In order to see how the text is organized, draw up a plan giving a heading to each paragraph or section and details of the points to be made in each. It might start like the one on the left, which just shows possible main headings.

Compare your completed plan with the example on page 90.

---

1 What ancient Egypt was like:

-
-
-

2 The problem that this caused the pharoahs:

-

3 What the pharoahs did about it:

-
-

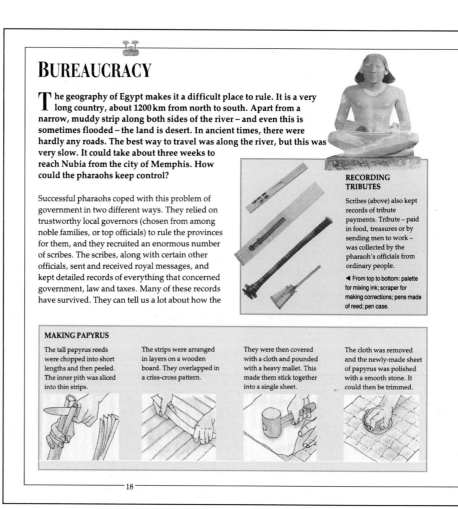

BUREAUCRACY

The geography of Egypt makes it a difficult place to rule. It is a very long country, about 1200 km from north to south. Apart from a narrow, muddy strip along both sides of the river – and even this is sometimes flooded – the land is desert. In ancient times, there were hardly any roads. The best way to travel was along the river, but this was very slow. It could take about three weeks to reach Nubia from the city of Memphis. How could the pharaohs keep control?

Successful pharaohs coped with this problem of government in two different ways. They relied on trustworthy local governors (chosen from among noble families, or top officials) to rule the provinces for them, and they recruited an enormous number of scribes. The scribes, along with certain other officials, sent and received royal messages, and kept detailed records of everything that concerned government, law and taxes. Many of these records have survived. They can tell us a lot about how the

RECORDING TRIBUTES

Scribes (above) also kept records of tribute payments. Tribute – paid in food, treasures or by sending men to work – was collected by the pharaoh's officials from ordinary people.

◄ From top to bottom: palette for mixing ink; scraper for making corrections; pens made of reed; pen case.

MAKING PAPYRUS

The tall papyrus reeds were chopped into short lengths and then peeled. The inner pith was sliced into thin strips.

The strips were arranged in layers on a wooden board. They overlapped in a criss-cross pattern.

They were then covered with a cloth and pounded with a heavy mallet. This made them stick together into a single sheet.

The cloth was removed and the newly-made sheet of papyrus was polished with a smooth stone. It could then be trimmed.

18

The design of the spread

Spreads in reference books often contain boxes of additional information and photographs with captions. Both are usually linked in some way to the main text.

FINDING THE DESIGN LINKS

1 Working with a partner, find three sentences or phrases in the main text which link up with the material in each of the three boxes.
2 Discuss what you have learnt from the illustrations which would have been hard to get across with writing alone.
3 Pick out any further activities which the information in boxes now permits you to do.

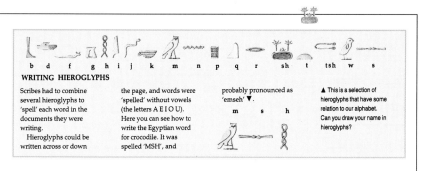

| b | d | f | g | h | i | j | k | m | n | p | q | r | sh | t | tsh | w | s |

WRITING HIEROGLYPHS

Scribes had to combine several hieroglyphs to 'spell' each word in the documents they were writing.

Hieroglyphs could be written across or down the page, and words were 'spelled' without vowels (the letters A E I O U). Here you can see how to write the Egyptian word for crocodile. It was spelled 'MSH', and probably pronounced as 'emseh' ▼.

| m | s | h |

▲ This is a selection of hieroglyphs that have some relation to our alphabet. Can you draw your name in hieroglyphs?

Egyptian government worked.

It took a long, slow training to become a scribe. Trainees started young – before they were 12 – and were made to work very hard while learning. Sometimes they were beaten – the Egyptians had a saying, 'a boy's book is on his back'.

Picture writing

Egyptian scribes wrote on paper called papyrus that was made from reeds. They used ink made of soot.

Sometimes they decorated their writings with red ink, as well. The Egyptian were among the earliest people in the world to invent writing, in around 3000 BC. They wrote using picture-symbols, known as hieroglyphs. Some hieroglyphs stood for the sounds that make up words, others stood for ideas, or for actual objects. For example, the hieroglyph for the sound we make when we say 'r' was an open mouth. The hieroglyph for the idea of drunkenness was a pot of beer.

▶ **Book of the Dead**
Egyptian scribes wrote many books, which have been preserved in the dry desert air. This page comes from a Book of the Dead. The picture shows a king (on the far right) making offerings to the gods. The writing describes how funeral ceremonies should be performed, and what each stage in the ceremony means. Books like these provide valuable evidence about Egyptian hopes, fears and religious beliefs.

19

Step 5:
Finding more information

If you wanted to find out more about the subject, the next step would be to check the Index once more. You could then turn to another book which looks useful and go through Steps 1 to 4 again.

Reading Language Signposts

As you have seen, a well designed page in an information book will give you a great deal of help, guiding you from one section to another. The same applies once you begin to look at the ideas in a particular article. It is very important to give the reader some 'signposts' in a piece of writing which will help them to understand how one idea is linked to another.

There are many common words and phrases which do this connecting job. They include expressions such as: 'As a result', 'However', and 'In the first place'.

One of the commonest signposts is 'For example', which tells the reader that there is an example coming up of a general point that has just been made. You can see how it can be used by looking back at the last section of the article on page 65.

Conjuncts

These connecting phrases are known as **conjuncts**. The word is very similar to conjunction (a word class which you learned about in Book 1, Unit 4). Both conjuncts and conjunctions perform the task of linking things together. Conjunctions link words or groups of words within the sentence. Conjuncts link paragraphs or sections of a piece of writing to show how they are connected in meaning.

There are many other kinds of conjuncts that writers can use. Examples of these are highlighted in this article on the Rosetta Stone. The functions of the conjuncts in the opening two paragraphs have been explained.

LANGUAGE DATABASE

▶ **Conjuncts**

Words or phrases which make it clear how one idea in a piece of writing or speech is linked to another:
e.g. It was cold and wet. *However*, we decided to grit our teeth and march on.
For more on conjuncts see pages 84-85 of The Reference Section.

EXPLAINING THE CONJUNCTS

In a group of three, discuss what jobs the other conjuncts perform in this article.
Which one:
- shows a link to do with time
- shows that a point is to be added
- shows that something happened as a result
- shows that the sentence is taking a different direction or that a problem is about to be raised?

The Rosetta Stone

Archeologists knew about Egyptian hieroglyphic writing for centuries. **However**, they were unable to decipher it until the Nineteenth century, when some of Napoleon's soldiers discovered a black stone at Rashid (or Rosetta). There was great excitement when it was discovered that the stone was carved in three different scripts. **First** there was a section in hieroglyphics; **then** one in the Egyptian 'demotic' script, used for everyday purposes; and **lastly** there was ancient Greek.

In addition, it was clear that the three sections were all about the same subject. It was easy to translate the Greek and this provided the key to the other scripts. **Nevertheless** it was some time before the demotic and hieroglyphic sections were fully deciphered. **Finally** a Frenchman called Champollion published a complete translation. **Consequently**, archeologists were able for the first time to understand fully the hieroglyphic inscriptions in temples and tombs throughout Egypt.

Tells us that this sentence is going to take a 'different direction' from the previous one, perhaps raising some kind of problem.

Tells us that there will be at least one other point after this one.

We can still expect another point.

This is going to be the final point in this 'set'.

LANGUAGE IN USE

1 Create a classroom display about 'Early Writing Systems'. If necessary, do some more research in your library. It will probably be best for you to work individually, each person taking one aspect of the subject. You might choose to produce a section on:
   - features of individual systems (such as Egyptian hieroglyphics or early American systems)
   - illustrations of different systems (including the very earliest cave inscriptions)
   - examples of different writing methods (making your own cuneiform clay tablet, for example, or scratching runes onto wood and stone)

2 Use what you have learned about early writing systems to produce an information sheet for the Year 6 class of your local primary school. The topic could be 'Ancient Writing' in general or something more specialized, such as 'Hieroglyphic Writing.'
   You could possibly explain how to produce your own cuneiform printing, using a wedge-shaped pen on clay or Plasticine. Remember who your audience are and use appropriate language and illustrations.

Stories in Performance

In Book 1, Unit 7 you heard Rik Mayall bringing a written story to life by his skilled performance. Now listen on the cassette to Victoria Wood telling a theatre audience her own story about her trip to work.

The Journey to Work

I've only just got here. I set off in my car this morning [whoosh!] down the motorway. I was stopped on the hard shoulder and this police car pulled up behind me. He said, 'Why have you stopped, madam?'

I said, 'I was just listening to *The Archers*.'

He said, 'I didn't hear that, madam.'

I said, 'Oh, didn't you? They're having terrible trouble with the pigs at Grange Farm.'

And he got cross and he checked my whole car over. He said to me, 'Your tyres are getting a bit bald. You'll have to get new ones.'

I said, 'Well, can't I do a sort of Robert Robinson and just comb the rest of the rubber over?'

Then he gave me one of those on-the-spot penalties that they've just started doing. I had to eat three cream crackers with a glass of water on my head.

So I set off, I set off, and I came off the motorway and I thought, well, I'll stop for a meal at one of those fast food places. [Gasp] God, it was like watching an action replay of a bowls match. The waiter – it would have been quicker to get served, it would have been quicker to raise the *Titanic* and see if there was any food left in the restaurant. This waitress, she came over and I said, 'I'll have beans on toast.' I could see her in the kitchen through the swing doors. She was staring at this loaf of bread... She was looking for the instructions... And she brought this beans on toast, freezing cold with a skin on the top. I said, 'Do you mind if I take this off, make a handbag?' I felt sorry for her being so slow, I tipped her a quid. By the time she picked it up, it was only worth seventy-five pence. Somebody came running in. They said, 'I think your car's been stolen!'

I said, [Gasp] 'No! What about my collection of insects?'

And they said, 'Where were they? On the back seat?'

I said, 'No. They were all stuck to the number plate.'

Victoria Wood

TALKING ABOUT HUMOUR

First of all, talk to a partner about the parts of Victoria Wood's anecdote which you found funny. Were they the same parts or are you amused by different things?

Think about two of the different kinds of humour found in Victoria Wood's story-telling.

Humour in unexpected comparisons

A number of her jokes are funny because she compares one thing with something else rather unexpected or silly. For example, it is funny to think that you could deal with a 'bald' tyre in the same way as some men try to cover up a bald head!

What does she make us compare each of the following with?

(The quotations in brackets show you where to look.)

- a traffic fine ('I had to eat three…')
- slow service in the restaurant ('God, it was like…')
- the skin on the cold baked beans ('I said, "Do you mind if…?"')

Humour in misunderstandings

There are also points in the story when one person misunderstands another.

Can you explain the misunderstandings when:

- the policeman says, 'I didn't hear that, madam.'
- she says, 'What about my collection of insects?'?

If you are feeling particularly clever, you might try to make up an anecdote of your own which includes both the humour of unexpected comparisons and the humour of misunderstandings.

For example, you might write about one of your first lessons in a practical subject like Science or Home Economics. What unexpected things happened? Which new expressions or terms led to humorous misunderstandings?

Telling a Good Story

The version of Victoria Wood's story printed on page 68 is called a **transcript** – a word-for-word *written* record of something that was originally *oral* (or spoken).

HEARING THE HUMOUR

Listen to the cassette again in pairs and list all the things that Victoria Wood was able to do in order to make the story funny and interesting for her *listening* audience, which she could not have done if she had decided to write the story down for people to read.

You may find it useful to turn back to Book 1, pages 64-65 and remind yourself of some of the advantages of oral story-telling. When you have made your list, compare it with the one on page 90.

Differences between speech and writing

There are some important differences between the language we use in speech and the language we normally use in writing.

DIFFERENT SENTENCES

When you look at the transcript of a spoken story, the sentences seem much more 'broken up' and disjointed than the sentences that we carefully put together when we write.

Find examples in Victoria Wood's story of each of these which are very common features of speech:

● repeating a phrase
● starting a new sentence without finishing the old one
● using the pronoun next to the noun it stands for

DIFFERENT EXPRESSIONS

There are many expressions which are often heard in speech, but are not normally used in writing.

For example, Victoria Wood says '...*this* police car pulled up...'. When someone is telling us a story, we do not look round in surprise and say 'W*hich* police car?'. We know that people often use *this* in spoken stories to mean simply *a* or *the*.

In your pairs, find three other examples in the transcript where *this* is used in that special way.

DIFFERENT VOCABULARY

We also use much more informal language in speech and this will often include slang words, as well as phrases such as 'sort of'.

1　Victoria Wood uses slang once in her story. Find this slang word and say which word you would use in more formal speech or writing.

2　How does the use of 'sort of' actually help to get the meaning across? Compare all your findings with the checklist on page 91.

For more on slang turn back to pages 26-27 in Unit 3.
You can hear Victoria Wood talking about joke-writing and the material in her sketches on the cassette.

'SPOKEN' LANGUAGE IN WRITING

Although there are great differences between the language we speak and the language we write, novelists and short story writers some-times choose deliberately to make the writing sound like the narrator's natural speech. For example read this opening from the novel, *Isaac Campion*.

Now then, I was twelve, rising thirteen, when our Daniel got killed. Aye… it was a long time ago. I'm talking about a time of day eighty-three years back. Eighty-three years. It's a time of day that's past your imagining…'

Janni Howker

We know this is from a novel. But which features of the language could make us believe that it was actually a transcript of an oral story? Make a note of some examples and share them in a class discussion. Look for instances where the writer:
- uses the old man's regional dialect rather than Standard English
- makes the speech sound slow and thoughtful
- gives the impression that Isaac is really talking to someone in particular.

If you are going to write a story in this way, it is not enough merely to copy out a transcript of a recorded oral one. It has to be worked on very carefully. Making writing sound like natural speech is not as easy as it sounds! (There is another example of Janni Howker writing in this way on page 73.)

Direct and Reported Speech

Very often when we are telling a written or spoken story, we decide to use the characters' actual words. For example:

> He said to me,
> *'Your tyres are getting a bit bald.'*

When we repeat the speaker's actual words we are using **direct speech**.

Sometimes, we decide to report what the person said, but not give the actual words. For example, Victoria Wood might have said:

> He *told me that my tyres were* getting a bit bald.

And, if we were retelling her story, we might write:

> He *told her that her tyres were* getting a bit bald.

Both of those sentences are examples of **reported speech**.

WORKING ON SPEECH

Think of some things that you have heard people say recently. First write out their exact words in direct speech; then write them out as reported speech. Work on five sentences from five different people.

You might find it helpful to study page 86 of The Reference Section, which looks in greater detail at the differences between *direct speech* and *reported speech*.

Direct Speech in Fiction

 Most story writers use much more direct speech than reported speech. For example, here is an extract from another story by Janni Howker, also to be found on the cassette.

The Nature of the Beast

And the headline was DOUBLE TRAGEDY FOR LOCAL FARMER.

'Here. Listen to this,' said Dad. 'You know Harry Fletcher up Hardale way, who Bill Howgill used to work for?'

'Aye,' said Chunder. 'What about him?'

'Seems like he lost damn near half his ewes in that blizzard.'

'That's a bad do,' said Chunder.

'And that's not all,' said Dad. 'Seems like he lost another two sheep to this here sheep-worrier. This dog. Says here he'd never seen anything like it. It had eaten lamb right out of one ewe and broken the back of the other. It was still alive when Harry found it. Had to shoot that one, it says here.'

'Must be a bloody big dog,' says Chunder. 'Here. Let me have a read.'

'Wait on. Wait on,' says Dad. 'Let me just find out who won the darts match.'

Janni Howker

There are at least three reasons why direct speech is effective here.

- We can 'hear' the characters' dialect (e.g. *Aye... That's a bad do... It had eaten lamb...*).
- We can hear the natural way in which people repeat things in normal conversation (e.g. *...to this here sheep-worrier. This dog...*).
- The direct speech enables us to see how quickly Dad's attention moves from one subject to another (from the horror of the sheep-killing to the 'more important' matter of who won the darts!).

All of this would be much harder to achieve through reported speech.

REASONS FOR DIRECT SPEECH

1   In groups of four, have a 'brain-storming' exercise to see how many reasons you can think of for using direct rather than reported speech in a story. Make a note of these.

 2   Look at extracts A, B, and C on page 74 and try to say why the writer might have chosen to use direct speech in each case.
You ought to be able to find more than one reason for each example. It may also help to listen to the readings of these on the cassette.

A

The Machine Gunners

A group of children in the Second World War are arguing about whether they had just seen a real machine-gun firing or not...

'You can't believe what's on *films*. Wasn't a real machine-gun.'

'Was. It was flashing.'

'Wasn't.'

'Was.'

'Wasn't.'

'What about that hole in the roof? And I'm not going back into the camp to make tea until you put that nasty great thing away.'

'SHURRUP.'

Robert Westall

B

The Owl Service

Alison is lying in bed ill. Suddenly she calls urgently to Gwyn downstairs...

'Gwyn!'

'Yes? What's the matter? You O.K.?'

'Quick!'

'You want a basin? You going to throw up, are you?'

'Gwyn!'

He ran back. Alison was kneeling on the bed.

'Listen,' she said. 'Can you hear that?'

'That what?'

'That noise in the ceiling. Listen.'

The house was quiet. Mostyn Lewis-Jones was calling after the sheep on the mountain: and something was scratching in the ceiling above the bed.

'Mice,' said Gwyn.

'Too loud,' said Alison.

'Rats, then.'

'No, listen. It's something hard.'

Alan Garner

C

The Cartoonist

Alfie loves to sit peacefully in his attic room, drawing cartoons, but his mother is always interrupting him...

He twirled the pencil, baton-like in his fingers. His thin fingers handled the pencil skilfully, and he began to draw again. He sketched lightly this time.

'Alfie!'

'In a minute.'

'Right *now*.'

Suddenly the light went out in the attic. Alfie knew what had happened. His mother had pulled the extension cord out of the wall below.

'*Mom!*' he protested.

'Well, I want you to come down here,' she said.

'Mom, plug my light back in.'

Silence.

Betsy Byars

When you have finished, compare your comments with the ideas on page 91.

3 In pairs, look at the novels that you are reading at the moment and decide why the writers might have chosen to use direct speech in particular scenes.

USING BOTH FORMS

In this extract from *Danny The Champion of the World*, Roald Dahl has chosen to use direct speech nearly all the time. Interestingly, though, he has decided to include a small amount of reported speech towards the end.

Read the extract carefully and then answer the questions which follow. You might also listen to the reading on the cassette.

Danny The Champion of the World

Danny's father runs a small country garage. One morning they have a particularly obnoxious customer.

Mr Hazell had pulled up alongside the pumps in his glistening gleaming Rolls-Royce and had said to me, 'Fill her up and look sharp about it.' I was eight years old at the time. He didn't get out of the car, he just handed me the key to the cap of the petrol tank and as he did so, he barked out, 'And keep your filthy little hands to yourself, d'you understand?'

I didn't understand at all, so I said, 'What do you mean, sir?'

There was a leather riding-crop on the seat beside him. He picked it up and pointed it at me like a pistol. 'If you make any dirty finger-marks on my paintwork,' he said, 'I'll step right out of this car and give you a good .hiding.

My father was out of the workshop almost before Mr Hazell had finished speaking. He strode up to the window of the car and placed his hands on the sill and leaned in. 'I don't like you speaking to my son like that,' he said. His voice was dangerously soft.

Mr Hazell did not look at him. He sat quite still in the seat of his Rolls-Royce, his tiny piggy eyes staring straight ahead. There was a smug superior little smile around the corners of his mouth.

'You had no reason to threaten him,' my father went on. 'He had done nothing wrong.'

Mr Hazell continued to act as though my father wasn't there.

'Next time you threaten someone with a good hiding I suggest you pick on a person your own size,' my father said. 'Like me for instance.'

Mr Hazell still did not move.

'Now go away please,' my father said. 'We do not wish to serve you.' He took the key from my hand and tossed it through the window. The Rolls-Royce drove away fast in a cloud of dust.

The very next day, an inspector from the local Department of Health arrived and said that he had come to inspect our caravan. 'What do you want to inspect our caravan for?' my father asked.

'To see if it's a fit place for humans to live in', the man said. 'We don't allow people to live in dirty broken-down shacks these days.'

My father showed him the inside of the caravan which was spotlessly clean as always and as cosy as could be, and in the end the man had to admit there was nothing wrong with it.

Soon after that, another inspector turned up and took a sample of petrol from one of our underground storage tanks. My father explained to me they were checking to see if we were mixing some of our second-grade petrol in with the first-grade stuff, which is an old dodge practised by crooked filling-station owners. Of course we were not doing this.

Roald Dahl

ANALYZING THE SPEECH

1 In pairs, look carefully at the section in which Mr Hazell talks to Danny. Read out his conversation with Danny as though this were a play. How does the use of direct speech:
   ● help the reader to see the kind of person Mr Hazell is
   ● show the contrast between his rudeness and Danny's politeness?

2 Now look at the section of direct speech in which Danny's father talks to Mr Hazell. First pick out the clues which tell you how the two characters are either speaking or behaving. Then act it out.
   Which words, apart from 'dangerously soft' might you use to describe the way in which Danny's father addresses Mr Hazell?

3 Look again at the final section which begins 'The very next day...'. Pick out the direct speech and the reported speech.
   Can you say why the writer chose to put some of the dialogue in reported speech, when the most of the story is in direct speech?
   When you have discussed all of these questions, compare your ideas with those on page 91.

So the Head says to me...

There is an example of an anecdote told by a Year 8 student on the cassette.

You are going to produce a spoken and a written version of the same story, drawing on the information in this unit. The aim is that each one should display the special qualities of oral or written story telling.

Telling your own story

1 Think of something interesting that once happened to you. Try to find an amusing or exciting story that will contain plenty of dialogue.

2 When you have thought of a good story, look back to pages 70-71, to remind yourself of the things that you can do to make the telling of it effective. Then tell your story to a partner and listen to theirs, recording both on tape as you do so. Each story should last about a minute.

Writing a transcript

3 In pairs, make transcripts of the two anecdotes. Use the Victoria Wood transcript as an example of how closely you have to follow the spoken version. (You will need to spend some time on this stage.)

> '...says to me, 'Where do you think you're going?' So I said, 'Nowhere.'

4 Now discuss each other's stories. Which parts were most effective? Was there anything that ought to have been added or left out? Was there a satisfactory ending?

Drafting a written story

5 Redraft your transcript as a written story, following these steps.
- Change all the expressions which are acceptable in speech but not in writing.
- Make sure that you are writing in the complete phrases and sentences which are suitable for a written story rather than the 'broken' ones which are natural in speech.
- Change the order of some passages.
- Leave some out altogether and add others.

6 Then look at the dialogue. Do you need to change the 'balance' between direct speech and reported speech?

7 When you have done all that, look through the piece once more, to see whether there are any other changes that need to be made. Then write a final draft.

The Reference Section
of Book 2 is in
three parts:

Part 1
on pages 78-82
provides more
information about
the structure of words.

Part 2
on pages 83-86
tells you more about
sentences and grammar.

Part 3
on page 87
gives advice
about spelling.

Part 1: The Structure of Words

A mixture of names

As we saw in Unit 1, almost any area of England and English-speaking countries will have place-names which come from all three of these languages: Celtic, Old English, and Old Scandinavian, as this map shows:

Runcorn
(Old English for 'wide bay' or 'creek')

Skelmersdale
(Old Scandinavian for 'valley of a man named Skjaldmarr')

Stretton
(Old English for 'farmstead on a Roman Road')

Eccles
(Celtic for 'church')

Ormskirk
(Old Scandinavian for 'the church of a man named Ormr')

Crewe
(Celtic for 'weir' or 'fish-trap')

And what about the Romans?

The Romans

The Romans themselves did not have much influence on today's English place-names. They used their language (Latin) for official writing, but it was not the spoken language of country people and so it was not used to name local places.

Many place-names, though, include the word *-chester* or *-cester*, such as Manchester, Cirencester and Chester itself. This comes from an Anglo-Saxon word *ceaster* which meant 'Roman town' and itself came from the Latin word for a camp: *castra*.

A checklist of English place-name elements

Many of the common place-name elements that you met in Unit 1 are included in the list on page 79 as well as some new ones. The letters following in brackets show their origins, and are explained below.

● In pairs, try to think of place-names which contain some of the elements but which were not used as examples earlier in the book, e.g. 'combe' or 'hurst'.

As–	'eastern' (OE)		**ness**	'headland' or 'cape' (OS)
avon	'river' (C)		**Nor–**	'northern' (OE)
borough or			**Prest–**	'priest' (OE)
brough or **bury**	'stronghold' (OE)		**scar**	'rock' (OS)
burn or **bourne**	'stream' (OE)		**Ship–**	'sheep' (OE)
by	'farmstead' or 'village' (OS)		**stead**	'place' (OE)
chester or **caster**	'Roman town or fort' (OE) (from Latin)		**stoke**	'secondary settlement' or 'outlying farmstead' (OE)
cot	'cottage' (OE)			
combe	'valley' (OE)		**stowe**	'holy place' or 'meeting place' (OE)
dale	'valley' (OS)			
den	'valley' (or sometimes: pasture for pigs) (OE)		**Sur–, Sus–** or **Sut–**	'southern' (OE)
don	'hill' (OE)		**thorp**	'secondary settlement' or 'outlying farmstead' (OS)
–ea, or **–ey**	'island', or 'land near water or marsh' (OE or OS)			
folk	'people' (OE)		**thwaite**	'clearing' (OS)
ford or **forth**	'river crossing-place' (OE)		**toft**	'homestead' (OS)
ham	'homestead' or 'enclosure' (OE)		**ton** or **stone**	'farmstead' (OE)
head	'headland' or 'hill' (OE)		**West–**	'western' (OE)
hurst	'wooded hill' (OE)		**well**	'spring' (OE)
–ing–	'followers of' or 'family of' (OE)		**Whit–**	'white' (OE)
			wich or **wick**	'farm' (OE)
kirk	'church' (OS)		**worth**	'enclosure' (OE)
ley or **leigh**	'woodland clearing' (OE)			
low	'hill' or 'mound' (OE)			
mer, **mere**, **mar** or **more**	'lake' or 'pool' (OE)			

OE = Old English
C = Celtic
OS = Old Scandinavian

ENGLISH PLACE-NAMES ROUND THE WORLD

Place-names which were invented hundreds of years ago in Anglo-Saxon England can now be found throughout the world.
For example: Washington (USA), Melbourne (Australia) and Wellington (New Zealand).

Use an atlas to find others from as many different countries as you can and then try to work out their meanings.

Celtic place-names

You have already learned that many of the Irish, Scottish, and Welsh place-names come from the Celtic languages of the people who lived in the British Isles before the Romans arrived.

● Use an atlas to see how many of these place-name elements you can find in Ireland, Scotland, and Wales.

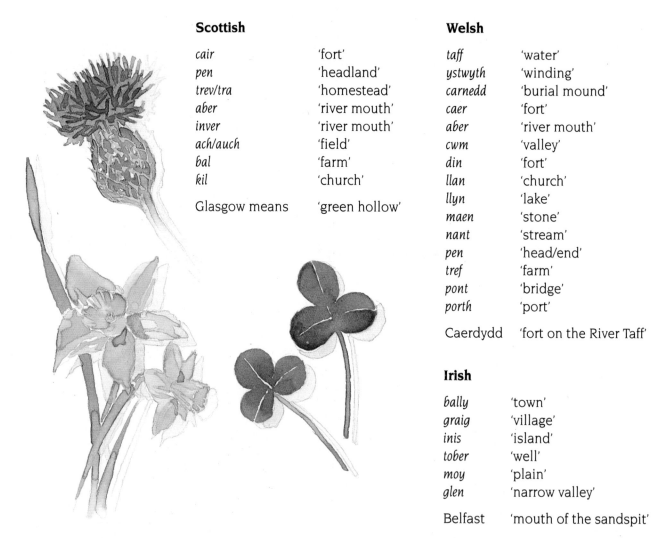

Scottish

cair	'fort'
pen	'headland'
trev/tra	'homestead'
aber	'river mouth'
inver	'river mouth'
ach/auch	'field'
bal	'farm'
kil	'church'
Glasgow means	'green hollow'

Welsh

taff	'water'
ystwyth	'winding'
carnedd	'burial mound'
caer	'fort'
aber	'river mouth'
cwm	'valley'
din	'fort'
llan	'church'
llyn	'lake'
maen	'stone'
nant	'stream'
pen	'head/end'
tref	'farm'
pont	'bridge'
porth	'port'
Caerdydd	'fort on the River Taff'

Irish

bally	'town'
graig	'village'
inis	'island'
tober	'well'
moy	'plain'
glen	'narrow valley'
Belfast	'mouth of the sandspit'

AND WHERE ON EARTH...?

Where and what are the following places? And what tells you that the last two were named only in the past thirty years?

Clavius   Lacus Somniorum   Mare Tranquillitatis
Gagarin   Apollo

Prefixes and suffixes

Prefixes and suffixes are groups of letters which are added to a word or part of a word to produce a new meaning.

Here is a list of the most common prefixes and suffixes. For each one, you have been given the meaning and an example.

These word-parts are more usually found as prefixes.

Prefix	Meaning	Example
ab	from, away	absence
ad	to, towards	advance
ambi/amphi	both	ambidextrous/amphibian
ante	before	ante-room
anti	against, preventing	anti-war; antiseptic
aqua	water	aquarium
audi/aur	hearing	audible/aural
auto	self	automatic
bene	well, good	benefit
bi/bin	two	bifocals, binoculars
bio	life; living things	biology
cent	a hundred	century
con/cor/ col/com/co	with	connect, correspond collect, compare, cooperate
demi/hemi/ semi	half	demigod, hemisphere semitone
duo	two	duet
ex (1)	out, away	exit
ex (2)	former, once	ex-president
extra	outside, beyond	extra-terrestrial
hydro	water	hydro-electric
hyper	over, excessive	hypertext
inter	between	international
kilo	thousand	kilometre
meta	change	metaphor
micro	small	micrometer
milli	thousand	millipede
mini	small	minibus
mono	one	monorail
multi	many	multiple
omni	all	omnibus
opti	seeing	optical
pan	all	panorama
photo	light	photo-sensitive
poly	many	polygon
post	after	post-war
pre	before	predict
pseudo	false	pseudonym
psycho	the mind	psychology
re	again	review

retro	back, backwards	retro-rocket
sub	under	submarine
super	above	supersonic
terra/terri	land	territory
theo	god	theology
trans	across	transatlantic
tri	three	triple
uni	one	unique
zoo	animals	zoology

These word parts are more usually found as suffixes.

Suffix	Meaning	Example
graph	written, recorded	photograph
logy	study of	geology
morph	form, shape	metamorphic
nomy	measuring	astronomy
ped/pod	feet	biped, tripod
scope	looking at	telescope

These word parts can be either prefixes or suffixes.

Prefix/Suffix	Meaning	Example
cycl	circle, around	cyclone, bicycle
metr/meter	measuring	metronome, centimetre
phon	sound	phonics, telephone
vor	eating	voracious, herbivore

NEW INVENTIONS!

Whenever people have needed to create a word to label a new invention or idea, they have turned to the old Latin and Greek prefixes and suffixes.

For example, the first people to invent a device that enabled us to hear recorded sounds joined *phone* (= 'sound') to *gram* (= 'written' or 'recorded'). The problem was, they could not decide at first whether the invention should be called a *phonogram* or *gramophone*!

Which new words did people create for the following:
- a form of transport with two wheels
- a creature with a hundred legs
- a device for measuring heat
- a device which picks up small sounds

Poetry and verbs

In Unit 5 you learned about the importance of nouns in poetry. Verbs are obviously important too, as they provide the 'action' of the poem. We can see this by looking at the verbs in Seamus Heaney's *Inishbofin*:

handed down... dipped and *shilly-shallied... sat* tight... nobody *speaking...* gunwales *sank* and *seemed* they might *ship* water...sea *was* calm... engine *kicked...* ferryman *swayed... reaching* for the tiller... I *panicked... guaranteed* us... *kept* me in agony... we *went sailing...* it *was* as if I *looked... sailing* through air... *could see..* we *fared... loved...*

 Which sounds or other sensations do you always associate with hot summer days? Make a list of them and then read this poem.

A Hot Day

Cottonwool clouds loiter.
A lawnmower, very far,
Birrs. Then a bee comes
To a crimson rose and softly,
Deftly and fatly crams
A velvet body in.

A tree, June-lazy, makes
A tent of dim green light.
Sunlight weaves in the leaves,
Honey-light laced with leaf-light,
Green interleaved with gold.
Sunlight gathers its rays
In sheaves, which the wind unweaves
And then reweaves – the wind
That puffs a smell of grass
Through the heat-heavy, trembling
Summer pool of air.

A. S. J. *Tessimond*

2   In the first line, the clouds are imagined as behaving like people. In other words, they are personified. Which verb shows us what they are doing and what does it seem to mean?

3   Both the sunlight and the wind are also personified. The verbs which show what the sunlight does are 'weaves' and 'gathers', as though it were a craftsperson of some kind. Pick out the verbs which show what the wind does.

4   Which words and phrases might be called onomatopoeic (see page 56)? Look at the ones which themselves seem to sound drowsy and warm. (Try reading out loud the phrase near the beginning which contains three adverbs.)

5   Write your own poem about a cold, rainy, or snowy day. You might find it interesting to use A Hot Day as a model, beginning with the sky, then a distant sound, then something happening closer. Think of the colours associated with the day and the way the weather affects the things that you can see, feel or hear.

Conjuncts

Conjuncts are the 'signposts' in a passage of writing which help to show how different parts of the passage are linked together. The conjuncts in the first half of the article on page 85 have been highlighted.

1   Try to describe how each one helps the reader to understand how one part of the article is linked to another. You may find it helpful to look back at the examples explained in the article on the Rosetta Stone on page 67.

2   Then see if you can pick out the conjuncts in the second half of the article and describe their functions. You will find a conjunct in each sentence. Compare your answers with the list on page 91.

When it comes to the question of UFOs, people seem to fall into one of two camps. Believers, **on the one hand**, claim that UFOs are simply the latest wave of visitors from space. Sceptics, **on the other**, argue that they can be explained in less dramatic ways. Their line is that weather balloons, **for example**, have often been mistaken for flying saucers. And that high-flying planes have also given rise to a lot of unwarranted excitement. **In addition**, there is a sky full of different weather conditions which can be extremely puzzling if you're not expecting them.

As a result, the average person's attitude to UFOs tends to be one of healthy cynicism.

All the same, there is no doubt that they are still capable of capturing the headlines and there are perhaps several reasons for this. Firstly, the public loves something out of the ordinary and there are few things less ordinary than a glowing cigar-shape in the night sky. Secondly, there is hardly anyone who would not love to believe that life exists beyond the earth; and UFOs are the nearest we ever get to proof. Finally, it has to be admitted that there are unexplained sightings. The problem with all of them, however, is lack of good documentary evidence.

Nevertheless while there are lights in the sky and romantic imaginations, UFOs will continue to grab the headlines. What is more, there is now a 'UFO industry' making a good deal of money out of magazines, books and UFO-spotters' specialist equipment.It seems then that, whether we like it or not, the UFO bug is here to stay.

3   In groups of four, discuss your attitude towards UFOs. Are you a Believer or a Sceptic, for example? Have you ever seen a 'flying object' which was never properly 'identified'? Do you know stories of people who have?

Direct and reported speech

This first passage of dialogue is in **direct speech**.
The speaker's actual words have been used:

> 'I've had enough. I'm packing it in,' said Charlie.
> 'Have you finished?' asked Miss Tomlinson, looking up from her book.
> 'I haven't finished,' said Charlie defiantly. 'I simply haven't got a clue what I'm supposed to be doing.'

Now read the same conversation, this time written in **reported speech**. The notes written around it show the main changes that are made when direct speech is written as reported speech:

The first and second person pronouns ('I', 'we' and 'you') change to the third person pronouns ('he', 'she' or 'they').

Words, such as 'whether' need to be added in reporting questions.

> Charlie said that **he had** had enough and **was** packing it in. Miss Tomlinson, looking up from her book, asked **whether** he had finished. Charlie **replied defiantly that** he **hadn't** finished and simply **hadn't** got a clue what he **was** supposed to be doing.

Verbs are usually 'shifted back' a tense, so that they change from present to past.

Reported speech tends to sound more formal.

1   Rewrite the next part of the conversation, shown here in direct speech, as reported speech:

> 'It's impossible,' he said.
> 'Have you read the instructions?' she asked.
> 'You haven't given me any.'
> 'You've left them on my desk. Come and collect them and then finish your work.'

2   Which other 'rules' have you now discovered to do with turning direct speech into reported speech? (At which points did you have to add phrases, for example? Which phrases did you choose?) Compare your version with the one on page 91.

Part 3: Spelling

The many uses of 'h'

In Units 1 and 2 you read about two letter patterns with the letter 'h':

1 **gh**, **ght**, (in words such as thou**gh**, thou**ght**).
2 **ch**, which can make a 'hard' sound in words such as s**ch**olar, **ch**emist, a**ch**e, te**ch**nology; or a 'soft' sound, as in **ch**urch, hit**ch**, **ch**arm.

'H' can also be found in these patterns:

3 In **th**, **the**
   e.g. clo**th**, ba**the**.
4 At the beginning of syllables before a vowel:
   e.g. **h**at.
   Sometimes this might not be the first syllable of a word:
   e.g. be**h**ind.
   And sometimes the h in the middle of a word makes it look rather odd.
   ● Use a dictionary (or ask your teacher for help) to check the meaning and pronunciation of ab**h**or and mis**h**ap.
5 Silent, in exclamations:
   e.g. A**h**! O**h**!
   ● Decide how **Eh** should be pronounced. When is it used and what punctuation mark usually follows it?
6 Silent, after **r**.
   e.g. **rh**ythm, **rh**inoceros.
   ● Which **rh** words mean 'a bunged up nose', and 'a diamond shape'?
   All of these are from Ancient Greek.
7 Silent, after **ex-** .
   e.g. ex**h**aust, ex**h**ibition, ex**h**ilarate (but it is pronounced in ex**h**ale)
   ● What does the prefix ex- mean? Check on page 81.
8 Silent, in some words which have been borrowed from French (in which h is never pronounced).
   e.g. **h**eir, **h**onest, **h**our.
   ● Which other words are there in the **hon-** family?
9 Silent, after **t**.
   e.g. **Th**ames, **t**hyme and (usually) Ant**h**ony.
10 After **w**.
   e.g. w**h**at, w**h**ere, w**h**y.
   ● In your accent do you say *wot* or do you blow slightly through your lips as you make the **w** sound?
11 After **p** to make an **f** sound.
   e.g. **ph**otograph.
   ● How many other **ph** words do you know?

Answers

What do they mean? (page 6)

Castleton is 'the farmstead by the castle'

Kingsbridge was named after an Anglo-Saxon king

Otterburn is 'the stream frequented by otters'

Southchurch is 'the southern church'. Perhaps there were several churches in that area

Draperstown gets its name from the Company of Drapers (cloth-sellers) who settled there

Ravenscar is 'the rock frequented by ravens'

Newquay was named after the new quay built there in the Fifteenth century

Greenford is exactly what it says: perhaps the ford was covered in moss or overgrown with vegetation

Wallsend was built at the end of Hadrian's Wall

Working out the meanings (pages 8-9)

2 **Prestwich** is 'priest farm'; **Whitby** is 'white stronghold'; **Shipley** is 'sheep clearing' (or 'pasture'); **Langdon** is 'long hill'; **Norfolk** is (the territory of the) 'northern people'; **Boroughbridge** is 'bridge near the stronghold'; **Swinstead** is 'pig homestead' (a homestead where pigs are kept); **Birmingham** is 'Beorma's family's homestead'.

3 **Ottery Saint Mary** in Devon gets its name from the church of St Mary, built by the River Otter (a 'stream frequented by otters'). **Toller Porcorum** in Dorset gets its name from the River Toller (a Celtic name meaning 'hollow stream'). **Porcorum** is Latin for 'of the pigs' as the village once had herds of swine. **Eye** is from an Anglo-Saxon word for an island or piece of dry ground in a marsh. There is an Eye in Cambridgeshire, Suffolk, and Hereford and Worcester.

A magic charm (page 10)
The translation from Old English is:
Out little spear, if it is in here!
If you were shot in the skin,
or were shot in the flesh,
or were shot in the blood…
If it were the shot of elves,
now will I help you.

Suffix-phobia (page 13)
Missing suffixes: ManagING DirectOR delightED PrintER completeLY reliABLE importANT busiNESS successFUL famOUS finALLY fanatIC informATION technOLOGY photoGRAPH newEST equipMENT faithFULLY

Looking at the structure (page 19)
A plan for the Oscars news item might look like this:
Para 1: Introduction – Main point of the item:
BRITAIN'S SUCCESSES IN THE OSCAR AWARDS.

Para 2:   (i) Main example – Emma Thompson
             (ii) quote from her
Para 3:   Two other examples – *The Crying Game* and Tim Rice
Para 4:   The other major interest – Clint Eastwood

Shakespeare's verbs (page 22)

break off; You are a scholar; Doesn't it look like (or does it not look like) the king? It would like (or wants) to be spoken to; What are you....? who usurp... Used to march; I charge (or command) you to speak.

UNIT 3

Using formal and informal speech (page 25)

Formal speech situations might include:
- giving a prepared talk to the class
- going for an interview
- debating

Informal speech situations might include any occasions on which you were being relaxed with friends.

In some situations it is difficult to know whether to use formal or informal speech. For example:
- answering a question in class
- giving directions to someone in the street
- speaking to an adult who you don't know very well

Who uses it? (page 27)

3   The differences between *slang* and *dialect*: There are two major differences.
- Regional dialect expressions have been around for a long time (whereas most slang goes in and out of fashion).
- Regional dialect expressions are also heard only in a particular region.

How does it work? (page 28)

2   Here is a written version of the conversation 'Would You Adam and Eve It?' from the cassette and the 'translation' of the rhyming slang used. 'Would you Adam and Eve it? I gave me Blackadder to a Brussels sprout to climb through me burnt, and 'e 'alf-inched the custard!' ''E's a right little tea-leaf, isn't 'e? D'you reckon 'e was short of bread?' 'No idea. I just want to see him up before the Barnaby and in the jug.'
Adam and Eve – believe; **Blackadder** – ladder; **Brussels sprout** – scout; **burnt** – from 'burnt cinder' window; **half-inch** – pinch; **custard** – from 'custard and jelly' telly; **tea-leaf** – thief; **bread** – from 'bread and honey' money; **Barnaby** – from 'Barnaby Rudge' (a character in a Charles Dickens novel) judge; **jug** – from 'jug and pail' jail

New rhyming slang (pages 28-29)

Michael Caine = a pain; **Glenn Hoddle** = a doddle; **Dudley Moore** = sore; **Cilla Black** = back; **Bugs Bunny** = money; **Vincent Price** = ice; **Popeye the sailor** = tailor; **Jeremy Beadle** = needle; **Kenneth Branagh** = spanner.

UNIT 4

What happens next? (page 38)
The children decide to do a project on Granny and the way in which she is treated in their household. They will then threaten to hand this in for homework and cause their parents enormous embarrassment unless they agree to let Granny stay at home.

Stage directions and tenses (page 40)
Verbs in the present tense were:
He **hangs**; Henry **goes**; They **are...sunk**; Ivan **claps**; They quickly **form**... and **sit** down; Sophie **is sunk**; Light **dawns** and she **lifts** her head.

UNIT 6

Choosing the references (page 63)
It might be worth looking up these further references:
archaeology, artists, crafts, hieroglyphs, papyrus, scribes, and temples.

Reading the main text (page 64)
Your plan might have included the following main points:

1 What ancient Egypt was like:
  ● a very long country
  ● most of it desert
  ● travel very slow
2 The problem that this caused the pharoahs:
  ● how to keep control
3 What the pharoahs did about it:
  ● governors ruled the provinces
  ● they recruited many scribes
4 The scribes' jobs:
  ● sent royal messages
  ● kept detailed records
5 The scribes' training:
  ● took a long time
  ● were often beaten
6 Their picture-writing:
  ● the materials:
    – wrote on papyrus
    – used ink made of soot
  ● invented around 3000 BC
  ● used hieroglyphs

UNIT 7

Hearing the humour (page 70)
Victoria Wood uses:
● sound effects (e.g. the whoosh of the car on the motorway)
● an imitation of the way people speak (e.g. the policeman)
● gasps of surprise (e.g. 'God, it was like...' 'No! What about my collection?')
● pauses (e.g. 'She was staring at this loaf of bread... She was looking for the instructions...')
● changes of pace: sometimes the dialogue speeds up, or slows down

Different sentences, expressions, and vocabulary (pages 70-71)
A Speech versus Writing Checklist
Someone telling a story will often:
- repeat phrases ('So I set off, I set off…')
- interrupt themselves and start a new sentence without finishing the old one ('The waiter - It would have been quicker…')
- include the pronoun as well as the noun ('This waitress, **she** came over…')
- use 'this' for 'a' or 'the' ('This waitress… this loaf… this beans on toast…')
- use slang ('I tipped her a **quid**…' – instead of the more formal *pound*)
- 'sort of' suggests that it would be **like** the kind of thing that Robert Robinson would do, but obviously not exactly the same!

Reasons for direct speech (pages 73-74)
A: We hear the exact ways the children argue and emphasize particular words.
B: Nearly all the story (the narrative) is told through the direct speech. The short speeches also add to the tension and mystery.
C: The precise words of Alfie's argument with his mother show how she is unfair and is unable to discuss the issue. She can only tell him what to do.

Analyzing the speech (page 76)
1
- Roald Dahl uses direct speech so that we can actually hear some of Mr Hazell's unpleasant and violent language, ('…look sharp about it… keep your filthy little hands to yourself…give you a good hiding.').
- At one point Hazell rudely ends his order with the phrase 'd'you understand?' Danny doesn't understand and so asks politely 'What do you mean, sir?' (even addressing him as 'sir'.).
2   The clues are that Danny's father 'strode up to… the car and placed his hands on the sill and leaned in.' These were all things which show how angry he is and they are all designed to make Hazell angry. Also, when he speaks, Danny's father's voice is 'dangerously soft'. Notice how politely but firmly he addresses Hazell.
3   The reported speech is in the following phrases: '…and said he had come to inspect our caravan.'; 'the man had to admit there was nothing wrong with it.'; 'My father explained to me they were checking to see…'
Perhaps Roald Dahl decided to use reported speech for most of the inspectors' statements because there was no need to give an idea of their characters; and he wanted to give the general idea of the incidents rather than precisely what was said.

THE REFERENCE SECTION

Conjuncts and UFOs (pages 84-85)
The conjuncts used in the second half of the passage are as follows:
All the same, Firstly, Secondly, Finally, however, Nevertheless, What is more, then.

Direct and reported speech (page 86)
He said that it was impossible. She asked whether he had read the instructions. He replied that she hadn't give him any.
She said (or a phrase such as 'pointed out') that he had left them on her desk and asked him to come and collect them and then finish his work.

Glossary

Abstract noun the label given to something you cannot touch such as an emotion, feeling or idea. e.g. happiness, thirst, hour.

Accent the way in which we pronounce words. Our accent usually depends on where we were brought up or the people we have mixed with. See **Received Pronunciation.**

Adjective a word which helps to give more information about a noun or pronoun. e.g. His voice was *quiet* and *polite* and *firm*. The *dry, musty* leaves.

Adverb a word which helps to give more information about a verb or an adjective or another adverb. e.g. with a verb: They *gradually* rebuilt the bridge. e.g. with an adjective: It was *extremely* difficult. e.g. with another adverb: They worked *amazingly* slowly.

Alliteration the repetition of consonant sounds in order to gain a special effect. e.g. He clasped the crag with crooked hands.

Apostrophe a punctuation mark (**'**) which has two quite different uses:
to show that a **letter** or group of **letters** has been **missed out**. e.g. That's gristle! I've got it!
to show **possession** (or ownership). e.g. Sophie's idea was brilliant. The doctor's language was ridiculous. The witches' meeting was brief.

Audience the name we give to the people we expect to read our writing. A roadsign, notice or poster are written for a *public* audience. A letter is usually intended for a *private* audience. A diary is written for a *personal* audience.
See **Topic**, **Form** and **Purpose**.

Biography and **Autobiography** A biography is a book or article written about someone's life. In an autobiography you write about *your own* life.

Collective noun the label we give to groups or collections of people, things or animals. e.g. a hockey *team*, an *army*, a stamp *collection*.

Comma a punctuation mark (**,**) used to break up sentences and make them easier to understand.

Common noun the general label we give to people, things or animals. e.g. girl, greenhouse, gorilla.

Complex sentence
See **Sentence**.

Conjunct a word or phrase which shows how one idea in a piece of writing is linked to another. e.g. therefore, however, lastly, as a result. See pages 66-67 and 84-85; also **Conjunction**.

Conjunction words used to join parts of a sentence, phrases or single words. e.g. They froze *when* they saw the King's ghost. You go through Saint Looey *and* Joplin Missouri. See **Conjunct**.

Consonant the sounds we make by using parts of the mouth or throat to briefly stop the air. e.g. the first sounds in *bay, key, do, fee, go*. See **Vowel**.

Coordinated sentence
See **Sentence**.

Dialect the kind of English spoken by a particular group of people (very often linked to a region), which has its own words and expressions and its own special grammatical rules. See pages 18-19; also **Standard English dialect**.

Dialogue characters' spoken words in a story. See pages 42-43 and 72-74; also **Inverted commas**.

Direct speech a speaker's exact words reproduced in writing, usually with speech punctuation. e.g. He said, 'I didn't hear that, madam.' See pages 72-77 and 86; also **Reported speech**.

Etymology an account of the history of a particular word, including the language it came from and its original meaning. It is sometimes called the **derivation**. e.g. the etymology of 'Dictionary' is the Latin word *dictio* meaning 'a word'. See pages 8 and 13.

Exclamation mark a punctuation mark (**!**) used to end a sentence or a speech in a piece of dialogue if we want to show shock or urgency, that something dramatic is happening or that a command is being given.
e.g. Aaargh! Quick! He was never seen again!

Form the *kind* of writing we are reading or producing. e.g. letter, poem, list. We use different forms at different times.
See **Topic**, **Audience**, and **Purpose**.

Full stop a punctuation mark (**.**) used to show the end of any sentence which is not a question or an exclamation. Full stops are also used to show shortened forms of words e.g. Dr. G.C.S.E.

Homophone a word which sounds the same as another, but has a different spelling and meaning. e.g. *there* and *their* or *here* and *hear*.

Inverted commas sometimes called **quotation marks** or **speech marks** are used in the punctuation of speech.

Jargon the special words used by particular groups of people who share the same job or interest. e.g. drop-shot (in tennis or badminton), interface (in computers), pulsar (in astronomy). See pages 30-33.

Metaphor a way of comparing two things, but without actually using a word such as 'like' or 'as'. e.g. I've been trying to wade through your essay; he's a pain in the neck; time flew past. See page 53; also **Simile**.

Narrative writing or speaking which tells a story.

Noun the word in a sentence which labels a person, thing, feeling or idea. e.g. *Mary* had a little *lamb* whose *fleece* was white as *snow*.
Nouns can be **Singular** e.g. A *man* gave his *child* a *dog*. Or **Plural** e.g. *Men* gave their *children dogs*.
See **Common noun**, **Proper noun**, **Abstract noun**, and **Collective noun**.

Onomatopoeia a word or phrase whose sound gives a kind of echo of its meaning. e.g. bleat tinkle whispering wings See pages 56 and 83-84.

Oral spoken. We talk about oral and written story-telling.

Paragraph a block of sentences all linked together by one main idea or subject. e.g. the opening paragraph of 'Writing Systems' on page 59 contains four sentences, all linked by the idea of the purposes of writing.

Part of speech
See **Word class**.

Personification a special kind of **metaphor** in which an object or idea is described as though it were a person.
e.g. Cottonwool clouds loiter; the leaves… throw a tantrum.
See pages 53 and 83-84; also **Metaphor**.

Phrase a group of words which makes some sense, but does not contain a complete verb.
e.g. round the corner   singing songs
Danny the champion of the world.

Plural
See **Noun**.

Prefix a group of letters which we add to the beginnings of words to change their meanings. Prefixes which change a word's meaning to its opposite are called 'negative' prefixes.
e.g. *un*natural *il*legal *im*possible.
See pages 12 and 81-82; also **Suffix**.

Pronoun a word which can be used in place of a noun. e.g. she they we.

Proper noun the label we give to a particular person, thing or animal.
e.g. Adlestrop, Natasha, Persil, Hamlet.
Proper nouns always begin with a capital letter.

Punctuation the marks we use in writing to make it easier to read and understand.
See **Full stop**, **Question mark**, **Exclamation mark**, **Comma**, **Apostrophe**, and **Inverted commas**.

Purpose the reason we have for writing something. e.g. our purpose might be to describe, to provide information or to entertain.
See **Audience**, **Form**, and **Topic**.

Question mark the punctuation mark (**?**) used at the end of a sentence or a speech in dialogue to show that it is a question. e.g. 'Can we stop them?' Ivan asked. 'When shall we three meet again?'

Quotation marks
See **Inverted commas**.

Received Pronunciation the neutral accent that some people use rather than a regional accent.
See **Accent**.

Reported speech the words that a character in a story says, but reported by the narrator, rather than reproduced word-for-word.
e.g. He said that I would have to get new tyres.
See pages 72-77 and 86; also **Direct speech**

Rhyme the effect produced by using words which end with the same sound or similar sounds.
e.g. hands lands stands
See page 57; also **Rhyme scheme**.

Rhyme scheme the pattern of rhymes in a poem.
e.g. The Eagle has three lines which rhyme, followed by a second three which have a different rhyme. (This is sometimes described as a rhyme scheme of aaa bbb.)

Rhyming slang a kind of slang used by the Cockneys in London, in which a phrase is invented which rhymes with the word that it stands for.
e.g. Barnet Fair (hair), Rory O'Moore (door), whistle 'n' flute (suit).
Usually only the first part of the phrase is used.
e.g. I put on me whistle, combed me Barnet and walked out the Rory.
See pages 28-29 and 89.

Sentence a group of words which makes sense. Sentences always begin with a capital letter and end with either a full stop, question mark or exclamation mark. A **Simple sentence** says just one thing. e.g. Egypt is a very long country.
When we join two simple sentences with 'or', 'and' or 'but', we make a **Coordinated sentence**.
e.g. It is easiest to travel by river *but* this is slow.
When we use a different conjunction to show how the two parts of the sentence are joined in meaning, we make a **Complex sentence**.
e.g. Young scribes were punished *if* they made mistakes.

Simile a way of comparing things in an unusual or unexpected way, in which the writer uses the words 'like' or 'as'.
e.g. Strutting like fat gentlemen; as awake as a morning flower.
See page 52; also **Metaphor**.

Simple sentence
See **Sentence**.

Singular
See **Noun**.

Slang a special form of language used by particular groups in informal situations, sometimes to add vividness or humour.
e.g. bread (money), kip (sleep), lug-hole (ear).
See pages 26-29; also **Rhyming slang**

Speech marks
See **Inverted commas**.

Stage directions words or phrases in a playscript which help the reader to understand how the characters should speak or behave.
e.g. Doctor (*Filling in the form*);
Sophie (*Sarcastically*);
(A *pause. They are all sunk in thought.*)
See pages 40-41.

Standard English dialect the neutral dialect which is not spoken in only one part of the country. Standard English is the dialect that many people choose to use in formal situations or when they have to speak to a large number of people who may all have their own different regional dialects. It is the dialect used by news presenters, for example, and is the one understood by most English speakers throughout the world. It can be spoken in any accent. Most writing is in Standard English dialect. See pages 18-19.

Suffix a letter or group of letters added to the end of a word in order to change its meaning, or added to a 'root-word' in order to make a new word.
e.g. –able, –graph, –scope
See pages 13 and 81-82; also **Prefix**

Synonym a word which means the same or almost the same as another word. e.g. *large* is a synonym for big, *stormy* for tempestuous.

Tense the form of the verb which shows *when* something happens. Verbs can be in the **present tense** e.g. My gran *is* in there. Or in the **past tense** e.g. My gran *was* in there. Or the **future tense** e.g. My gran *will be* (or *is going to be*) in there.
See **Verb**.

Topic the subject that we choose to write about. The topics of the passages in this book include: Writing Systems, UFOs, and Golf. When we are planning a piece of writing, it is useful to draw up a **Topic web** (also called a **Spidergram**).

Transcript an exact word-for-word record of what a person actually said (with all the mistakes, hesitations and repetitions left in).
e.g. The waiter – It would have been quicker to raise the *Titanic*...
See page 77.

Verb the word in a sentence which enables us to say what people (or things) are doing or being.
e.g.I *remember* Adlestrop; the steam *hissed*; a blackbird *sang*. Some verbs are single words; others are **verb phrases**.
e.g. He *is leaving* today. She *might have arrived* early.
See **Tense**.

Vocabulary the words used in a piece of writing or speech. We might say that a 'Postman Pat' book uses simple vocabulary.

Vowel a speech sound we make when the air passes freely through the mouth and is not stopped by parts of the mouth or throat. e.g. the sounds in the middle of p*a*d, n*e*t, d*i*p, T*o*m, t*oo*k, m*u*d. Sometimes the letters a, e, i, o, u are themselves called the vowels.

Word class a group of words which do a particular job in a sentence. e.g. N*ouns* label people, things or ideas; *adverbs* tell us more about verbs. They are sometimes called **Parts of speech**.The word classes described in this glossary are **nouns, pronouns, adjectives, verbs, adverbs** and **conjunctions**.

Acknowledgements

The author and publisher are grateful for permission to reproduce the following copyright material:

BBC Enterprises: extract from 'Journey to Work' sketch in transcript and on cassette, from *Victoria Wood* (BBC Radio Collection, 1991). **British Library:** Contents and Index pages from A. Gaur, *A History of Writing* (1984). **Collins** (an imprint of HarperCollins Publishers Ltd): extract from *The Owl Service* (1967) by Alan Garner; extract from *The Granny Project* (Collins, 1986) by Anne Fine; extracts from *Isaac Campion* (Fontana Lions, 1986) and *The Nature of the Beast* by Janni Howker. **Faber and Faber:** for Seamus Heaney, 'Inishbofin' ('Seeing Things I') from *Seeing Things* by Seamus Heaney. **The Guardian:** extract from 'Alfredsson gets clear in the Open', 26 July 93. **The Independent on Sunday:** extracts from *The Independent on Sunday*, 25 July 1993. **Ruth Kingshott:** 'Senses' first published in *Young Words* (1987), subsequently in *On Common Ground*, ed. Jill Pirrie (Hodder, 1987), © W.H. Smith. **Macmillan:** extract from *Machine Gunners* (1975) by Robert Westall. **Oxford University Press:** extracts from *Hamlet*, Act 1 Scene 1, Oxford School Shakespeare (1992), ed. Roma Gill; *Macbeth*, Act 1 Scenes 1 and 2, Oxford School Shakespeare, 1977 (new ed. 1992), ed. Roma Gill; from *Oxford Children's Encyclopedia* Vol. 5; and from *A Dictionary of English Place-names* (1991), p.149, by A. D. Mills. **Murray Pollinger Ltd:** extract from *Danny The Champion of the World* (Jonathan Cape Ltd, 1975), (Penguin Books Ltd, 1977). **Quarto Publishing:** extracts from *Insights: Ancient Egyptians* (1992). Photos: Andrew Stewart/Cairo Museum. **Random House UK Ltd:** extract from *The Cartoonist* by Betsy Byars (Bodley Head, 1967); Richard Kell, 'Pigeons' from *Control Tower* (Chatto and Windus Ltd). **Routledge and Kegan Paul:** extract paraphrased from *Slang Today and Yesterday* by Eric Partridge (1970). **Scholastic Children's Books:** extract from *My Mate Shofiq* by Jan Needle (Andre Deutsch, 1978). **Usborne Publishing Ltd:** Contents and Index pages from the *Usborne Children's World History*, copyright © 1979 Usborne Publishing Ltd. **Warner Chappell Music Ltd and International Music Publications Ltd:** extract from *Route 66* lyrics in book and on cassette, by Bobby Troup.

Although every effort has been made to contact copyright holders prior to printing, in some cases no reply has been received. Any errors or omissions in the above list are entirely unintentional. If notified, the publisher will be please to rectify these at the earliest opportunity.

The publisher would like to thank the following for permission to reproduce photographs:

Allsport p.32; BBC, NCA Picture Library p.24; British Museum p.67; British Telecom p.13; James Davis Travel Photography p.15; Michael Holford Picture Library p.58; Life File/Dave Thompson p.25 (top left & bottom left), Life File/Mike Evans p.25 (centre), Life File/Nicola Sutton p.25 (right); Rex Features/Sipa Press p.19, Rex Features p.68, p.69.

The illustrations are by Michael Allport p.35, p.36, p.38, p.40, p.44, p.73, p.74; Juliet Breese p.13; Paul Fisher-Johnson p.17, p.18, p.71; Nicola Gregory p.7, pp.10/11, p.49, p.53 (bottom); p.80; David Loftus p.6; Mary Lonsdale p.50 (bottom), p.53 (top), p.83 (bottom); Zoé Pearson p.50 (top), p.52, p.57; Steve Rigby p.14, p.51, p.54, p.56; Julie Roberts p.12, p.41, p.82; Martin Sanders p.78; Adam Stower p.42, p.43, p.45, p.75, p.76, p.85; Jacqui Thomas p.30, p.31 (all), p.72 (bottom), p.77, p.87; Alex Tiani p.26, p.28, p.29 (left & right), p.70; Harry Venning p.20 (top & bottom), p.21, p.22, p.23, p.72 (top); Jason Walker pp.46/47.

Handwriting by Elitta Fell.

Oxford University Press, Walton Street, Oxford OX2 6DP

Oxford New York
Athens Auckland Bangkok Bombay
Calcutta Cape Town Dar es Salaam Delhi
Florence Hong Kong Istanbul Karachi
Kuala Lumpur Madras Madrid Melbourne
Mexico City Nairobi Paris Singapore
Taipei Tokyo Toronto

and associated companies in
Berlin Ibadan

Oxford is a trade mark of Oxford University Press

© John O'Connor 1994
First published by Oxford University Press 1994
Reprinted 1994

ISBN 0 19 831181 8

Printed in Italy.